WHAT ALL STOCK AND MUTUAL FUND INVESTORS SHOULD KNOW!

By Bruce Sankin

Copyright 1990, 1992, 2003, 2004 by Bruce Sankin.
Revised 1992, 2002, 2003, 2004, 2005
Published by: Bruce N. Sankin & Associates,
PO Box 77-1502, Coral Springs, Florida 33077
Library of Congress Catalog
Card number: 90-86108

FEB - - 2007

2

TABLE OF CONTENTS

About the Author 5

Preface 7

Chapter One
How to Save Money on Buying and Selling Stock..........9

Chapter Two
Bonds..13

Chapter Three
Mutual Funds 21

Chapter Four
How Important is the Account Form?....................29

Chapter Five
What You Should Know that Could Save You Money ..37

Chapter Six
Arbitration..43

Chapter Seven
Preparing for an Arbitration 49

Chapter Eight
Did You Buy Mutual Funds? 59

Chapter Nine
Arbitration Awards - Mutual Funds....................63

Chapter Ten
Arbitration Awards - Stocks and Options 91

Chapter Eleven
Were You Caught Up In Technology or the Internet Boom?.....99

Chapter Twelve
Mediation - Take Control Over the Outcome
of Your Dispute..105

Chapter Thirteen
Frequent Questions from Investors...........................113

Chapter Fourteen
Columns and Endorsements...............................127

Spanish Version...139

About the Author

Bruce Sankin is a former stockbroker, having worked for Prudential-Bache & Dean Witter. He has a Bachelor of Science degree in finance and was a member of the Law Society.

Mr. Sankin writes a column on arbitration and has been interviewed in many publications like Money Magazine and The Wall Street Journal. He has appeared on national television and has been used for his expert opinion in arbitration cases. He is also an arbitrator and mediator specializing in securities.

He currently is an investment counselor based in Coral Springs, Florida. In addition to writing for professional journals and researching for high quality investments, Mr. Sankin also advises individuals, pension plans, and corporations on mutual funds, CD's, bonds, and money market investments.

If you lost money on specific investments that you feel were unjustified, contact me and I will review your situation.

For more information, or if you have any comments about your own investment experiences that would be helpful to other investors, or if you would like to comment about the book, please write:

Bruce Sankin
PO Box 77-1502
Coral Springs, Florida 33077
954-346-8585
bruce@investorsrights.com
www.investorsrights.com

Know Your Rights as a 401k Investor

By Bruce Sankin, National Consumer Advocate on Investors Rights

If you are a participant in a 401k plan, it also means you are an investor. As an investor, you MUST become educated about your financial future! I am a financial author and columnist; in addition, I am a consumer advocate for investor's rights. It always amazes me how people who have 401k plans really do not take an interest in knowing their rights when it comes to their financial future.

Here is an example: If you go to a mall and buy a television, or clothes, or any other product and realize there is a problem with the product, you know exactly what your rights are and instinctively know what to do. You go back to the store with your receipt, tell the salesperson there is a problem, and ask for a refund. If the salesman says no you ask for the manager. If the manager says no you go all the way up the line until you get your money back. Yet, when it comes to your investments in your 401k plan, which could be tens of thousands if not hundreds of thousands of dollars, if there is a problem, most people do not know their rights or what to do. You MUST become an aggressive consumer with your investments the same way your are with other products and services!

Remember, after your physical health, your financial health is paramount!

What do I mean by being an aggressive consumer?
1.   Know all fees, performance data, and investment objectives before investing.
2.   Read prospectus before investing.
3.   Understand asset allocation and invest accordingly.
4.   Know exactly who to contact when you have questions about your 401k.

5.   If your investment objectives, or life situation changes (you get married, divorced, widowed, change jobs, etc.) review and alter investments to ensure they reflect new realities.

If you do not think being an aggressive consumer when it comes to your investments is important, here are some facts. At the National Association of Securities Dealers (NASD) investors who lost money and knew their rights and first mediated and then arbitrated, 91% got back part to all of their investment losses!

Be smart. Be wise. And be aggressive!

Plan administrators should also be communicating to their plan participants that since they own mutual funds, they need to become an educated, informed investor who knows their rights as an investor. Help arm them with the right questions.

Bruce Sankin, a consumer advocate and columnist, is the author of "What All Stock and Mutual Fund Investors Should Know!" The manual, which is used by state regulatory agencies, Division of Securities, and plan sponsors as an educational tool designed to enhance investor literacy. Mr. Sankin has set up a secure website where you can purchase this book at a substantial discount off of the price at Amazon and Barnes & Noble. http://www.investorsrights.com/401k/.
Bruce welcomes your financial questions which can be sent to: bruce@investorsrights.com.

CHAPTER 1

HOW TO SAVE MONEY ON BUYING AND SELLING STOCKS

A stockbroker receives a commission for the service of buying or selling your stock. If you want to know your commission cost before deciding to make a trade, just call your stockbroker and he will be able to give it to you. It should be noted that your broker has the authority to offer you a 5%-20% discount. However, most brokers will not volunteer this information, since it means that they will make less money from the trade. Therefore, if you want the discount you must ask your stockbroker for it.

It is not in the stockbroker's best interest to give you a large discount because some brokerage firms pay less of a commission to the broker if the discount exceeds a certain percentage. Stockbrokers work on what is called a "grid." The percentage of commission a stockbroker receives is dependent upon the amount of business the broker generates for the brokerage firm. For example, if the stockbroker is on a 35% payout grid, he is entitled to 35% of the commission that the brokerage firm charges you. If, however, the broker discounts a stock trade more than his firm permits, they may pay him less than 35% of the commissions.

Remember what your stockbroker does not want you to know, **BROKERAGE FIRMS WILL ALLOW LARGER DISCOUNTS**. Sometimes the broker will need his office manager's approval. Ask your broker to ask his manager for a larger discount. Many managers may not want you to know that the firm can offer a larger discount because managers receive a percentage of the total revenue the office generates, so larger discounts will mean less money for him.

If you want to buy 200 shares of stock at a price of $20.00 per share, the total cost would be $4,000.00 plus your stockbroker's commission. At a full service brokerage firm, the commission rate quoted by a stockbroker could be as much as 3.1% of the purchase price of the stock, or $125, in the above example. This is very expensive. Usually a fair price is considered to be between 1% and 2%. Thus, you can, and should, negotiate with your broker.

An alternative to negotiating with your broker over his commission is to tell your broker that you want to trade on a per share basis. Trading on a per share basis is when you pay a commission on each share of stock that you purchase as opposed to a percentage of the total purchase price of that stock, i.e. a commission. It is possible to negotiate a $.10 to $.25 per share cost with your broker. **Tell your broker what you are willing to pay him**. If your stockbroker tells you he will not do the trade at the commission cost you want, then find a broker who will. There will always be stockbrokers who are looking for business.

If you are directing the transactions in your account, i.e. telling your broker what to buy or sell, then his services are of limited value to you anyway since he is merely an order taker. Thus, you should have a say in deciding how much money his services are worth.

You must not forget that a stockbroker is a commissioned salesman; he wants and needs your business. Do not believe your broker if he says that he does not. **That is how he makes his living**. He does not want to lose your business or for you to get advice from anyone else. And, if your broker really does not want to do your trade at your price, do not worry, you will always find one who will, you just need to look.

CHAPTER 2

BONDS

If you ask, your stockbroker has to tell you his commission on a purchase or sale of a stock. Likewise, if you ask, he has to tell you the sales charge when you purchase or sell a mutual fund. However, when you want to buy a bond, whether it is a tax free municipal bond, most corporate bonds, or a treasury bond, your broker does not have to tell what he and the firm are making on the transaction. This is because bonds are bought and sold on a mark-up or mark-down basis and mark-ups or mark-downs do not have to be disclosed. Buying or selling a bond with a mark-up and mark-downs rather than commissions is called buying or selling "net".

If you go to your broker to buy a tax free municipal bond and he says the price is $10,000.00 net, he will generally tell you that the price includes commissions. You can however still find out what the cost to you of the transaction is by asking the broker what the firm would pay you if you wanted to sell the same bond to them. If, for example, the answer was that the firm would pay you $9,600.00 if they were buying it from you, then the actual cost (spread) of the bond is $400.00 or 4%.

If you ask your broker what the buying or selling price of a bond is, this price is usually on his computer. He can also wire or email his bond department to get the information. He also has other options. He can check his bond inventory on his computer. Brokerage firms keep an inventory of bonds to offer and sell to their clients. The potential problem is that bond prices could change daily. This means that the price of a specific bond could be different at different brokerage firms. Each brokerage firm charges a price they feel they can get for it. The difference between the bid and ask (sell and buy) given to the broker by the bond department is generally 1/4 to 1% spread. This spread is what the bond department makes on the bond. Then the stockbroker adds on his commission which will usually be between 1/2% and 4%. **What you, as the client, are probably unaware of is that the broker can mark up or mark down the bond depending on what he thinks you will pay for it or sell it for.** On a buy and sell of the same bond, the broker and the brokerage firm together could make as much as 6% on the trade.

What your stockbroker does not want you to know is that you can negotiate bond prices. When he gives you a price for a bond you can usually negotiate between 1/4% and 1% of the price of the bond. On a $25,000.00 purchase or sale, you could save as much as $250.00. If your broker does not want to give you this discount, then call other brokers and tell them what you are looking for. With billions of dollars of bonds for sale everyday, there will be a broker who can usually get your bond at your price. On the other hand, if your broker offers you a bond and, after calling other brokerage firms, you find it to be the best price, quote, and yield – **BUY IT.** Getting what you want is more important than knowing what the brokerage firm makes.

UNIT TRUSTS

In some instances brokerage firms or independent companies put a group of bonds together and sell them as a package. These packages are usually called "unit trusts". A unit trust may be preferable to individual bonds because it diversifies the risk among a group of bonds instead of putting all the money into one bond. Another benefit of the unit trust is that interest payments are made monthly as compared to an individual bond, where interest payments are made semi-annually. On the other hand, the cost of buying a unit trust is not cheap; it can range from 4% to 5% and is an integral part of the structure of the trust. Therefore, commissions on unit trusts cannot generally be negotiated. The purchase of unit trusts is, however, subject to commission discounts in the form of "break points". This means that for certain volume purchases the commission will decrease. Common breakpoints in the purchase of unit trusts are $50,000, $100,000, and $250,000.00. Under a $100,000 purchase you may pay 4¾% commission while at $100,000 you may pay 3¼%, at $250,000 2½% etc. (It should be noted that your broker receives a commission when you buy a unit trust, though not usually when you sell it.)

When you ask about a unit trust, your broker will give you three quotations. He will quote you the price that you will pay if you want to buy it (ask price); the price that you will get if you want to sell it (bid price); and the actual value (par value) of the bonds in each unit of the trust. The par value is also the amount of money you will get back if you hold each unit to maturity (or to the call date, if the unit is priced to call).

When your broker gives you a price and yield on a unit trust make sure he tells you two yields: the current yield and the yield to maturity or to call date. It is also important to find out if the bond in the unit trust has a call feature. This means that the company or municipality can buy the bonds back from the unit trust before maturity. It has no option if the bond gets called. The unit trust must sell it back. Make sure your broker tells you what the yield to call is. It could be a lot less than a yield to maturity or current yield and you do not want any surprises after you buy the unit trust.

Be very careful when your broker gives you a quotation for a current yield on a unit trust that seems higher than an individual bond. If this does occur, ask him for the bid price, the ask price and the par value. For example, if he tells you that you will get 7.75% current return on a unit trust and a comparable individual bond is only giving 7.0% current return, then there is a good chance you are paying a premium for each unit trust.

A premium is the difference between what you pay (ask price) and the actual value (par price). If the ask price for the unit is $1,000.00 per unit and the par price is $900.00 per unit, you are paying $100.00 per unit or 10% more than the actual value. If you bought 10 units at $1,000.00 each and paid $10,000.00 and you held the units to maturity, you would only get back $9,000.00. You would get more income on your units each year, but in the end you would get less principal back then you put in. Premium bonds and unit trusts can be a good investment as long as you understand what you are giving up in principal for the extra yearly income. When buying bonds you should ask your stockbroker about the rating of the bonds or unit trusts. A rating will give you the quality and risk of each bond. The higher the quality, the less the risk, the lower the yield or "return on your investment". Conversely, the lower the quality, the higher the risk, and the higher the yield. Most bonds are rated by two rating companies: Standard & Poors, commonly know as S&P, and Moody's Investor Service.

The following is Standard & Poor's definition on rating of bonds:

AAA -   Debt rated 'AAA' has the highest rating assigned by Standard & Poor's. Capacity to pay interest and repay principal is extremely strong.

AA -   Debt rated 'AA' has a very strong capacity to pay interest and repay principal and differs from the higher rated issues only in small degree.

A -   Debt rated 'A' has a strong capacity to pay interest and repay principal although it is somewhat more susceptible to the adverse effects of changes in circumstances and economic conditions than debt in higher rated categories.

BBB-   Debt rated 'BBB' is regarded as having an adequate capacity to pay interest and repay principal. Whereas it normally exhibits adequate protection parameters, adverse economic conditions or changing circumstances are more likely to lead to a weakened capacity to pay interest and repay principal for debt in this category than in higher rated categories.

BB, B, CCC, CC, C -

Debt rated 'BB', 'B', 'CCC', 'CC' and 'C' is regarded, on balance, as predominantly speculative with respect to capacity to pay interest and repay principal in accordance with the terms of the obligation. 'BB' indicates the lowest degree of speculation and 'C' the highest degree of speculation. While such debt will likely have some quality and protective characteristics, these are outweighed by large uncertainties or major risk exposures to adverse conditions.

Bond Investment Quality Standards:

Under present commercial bank regulations issued by the Comptroller of the Currency, bonds rated in the top four categories ('AAA', 'AA', 'A', 'BBB', commonly known as "Investment Grade" ratings) are generally regarded as eligible for bank investment. In addition, the Legal Investment Laws of various states may impose certain rating or other standards for obligations eligible for investment by savings banks, trust companies, insurance companies and fiduciaries generally.

There are also bonds known as nonrated or NR bonds. This means that for some reason S&P and/or Moody's have not rated the quality of that particular bond. It does not mean, however, that there is something wrong with the bond. If you are interested in a nonrated bond, ask your stockbroker to find out the reason why it is not rated. If there is not a good reason why the bond has not been rated, then the best thing to do is to pass on that bond and find another bond with a rating that meets your satisfaction.

Many unit trusts are sold in a secondary market. This means that an individual sold the unit trust before maturity. Often, Unit Trusts sold before maturity are purchased by the brokerage firm and put into the brokerage firm's inventory. This means that you may be able to buy a unit trust that has a higher coupon, (premium) or lower coupon (discount) from the brokerage firm's inventory.

Individual bonds and unit trusts have something in

common which buyers sometimes are unaware of. The face value of these investments is only paid at maturity. If you sold these investments before maturity, you would get the market value. Market value is the price the brokerage firm is willing to pay. This could be higher or lower than the amount you paid for it. Example: You bought a $10,000 General Electric bond that expires January 1, 2020. If you held the bond to maturity, General Electric would pay you $10,000 on January 1, 2020. If you sold this bond before January 1, 2020, it is strictly the brokerage firm's decision what price they will pay you for the bond.

CHAPTER 3

MUTUAL FUNDS

One of the largest groups of products in the 1980's, where retail brokers made enormous commissions, was in mutual funds. Mutual funds are a simple way to invest in securities. You tell your stockbroker what you are looking for: stocks; bonds; an aggressive or conservative investment strategy; an income or an appreciation approach; then your broker finds the mutual fund which fits your needs. Since your broker is probably a commissioned salesman, he will usually attempt to sell you an open ended mutual fund that has a "load" or sales charge. Most stock funds with front end loads have sales charges between 4% and 8½%. Bond funds have sales charges that range between 3% and 5%. Sales charges are usually reduced the more you invest. This is known as "break points" or, in simple terms, a volume discount.

In the early 1980's brokerage firms and mutual fund companies realized people did not like to pay an upfront sales charge, so they invented a new type of sales charge called "backend sales charge", or "redemption fees". This means that you may pay a sales charge when you sell your shares back to the fund. Most backend load mutual funds have an additional annual expense to the shareholder known as the 12b-1 fee. Mutual fund managers say this fee is used to promote and advertise the fund to other potential shareholders. This fee can be as high as 1¼% per year. If you hold a mutual fund that has a 12b-1 fee of 1.25% for ten years and then sell it, you will be giving up an additional 12½% of your assets. 12b-1 fees of less than ¼ of 1% a year really do not make a great difference; however, anything more than that, unless the fund is a stellar performer, is unjustified in my opinion and I would look for another fund.

Stockbrokers do not want you to know that you do

not have to buy mutual funds from stockbrokers. If you care about what happens to your money and are willing to put in the hours of research to oversee your finances, you can buy no load mutual funds. There are many no load mutual funds with the same or similar types of securities and investment objectives that your broker would purchase for you with a sales charge, known as a load. If you have $10,000.00 to invest, one option would be to call up you stockbroker and set up a meeting. At that meeting, you could discuss your financial needs. At the end of the meeting, after the stockbroker did his due diligence he would probably recommend a specific mutual fund. If that mutual fund has a sales charge of 5% you have just paid him $500.00 for his professional financial advice. You now have to decide if your face to face meeting was worth it. Once the money goes into the mutual fund, performance is up to the portfolio manager.

IMPORTANT! - What is very important is that unless you know, and understand, how to select a no load mutual fund which meets your risk tolerance, investment objective, and suitability, you might be emotionally induced by the wrong factors to purchase a specific mutual fund. Unfortunately, many average and unsophisticated investors purchase a mutual fund based on its latest twelve-month performance without considering those other factors. Since we are talking about large amounts of money that could affect your financial future, unless you are willing to put in the time, effort, research, and monitoring of your money, the services of a qualified financial professional may be the better value.

If you decide to choose a mutual fund yourself, there are a number of sources you can use. One of the best sources is the **Morningstar Mutual Funds Value Report.** This book will give you the information you will need to make a fair judgement on thousands of mutual funds. Many stockbrokers use this information in choosing mutual funds for their clients. Magazines like **Money** and **Forbes** publish special editions that describe and rate mutual funds. There are also newsletters that follow the mutual fund industry.

Check Internet search engines for "Mutual Fund Newsletters" Monthly newsletters give recommendations and updates on most mutual funds.

If you don't want to put in the time and effort to find a no load fund and still want to use the services of a stockbroker to recommend a good family of funds, here is an idea on how to reduce the sales charge. Many excellent families of funds like M.F.S., Putnam, Delaware Group, American, Aim, etc. have different funds within the same family. All of these funds have exchange privileges, which means you can switch from one fund to another at net asset value. What your stockbroker doesn't want you to know is that different funds within the same family have different sales charges. This means you can buy a fund that has a load of 2½% and a week later you can exchange it for a fund you really wanted, which has a 5¾% load saving you 3¼% on the purchase of the fund. This could be hundreds of dollars or more in savings you don't have to pay your broker. These savings will range from 25%–60% of the sales charge. There are two types of mutual funds: open-end and closed-end. Open-end mutual funds consist of a portfolio of securities that trade at net asset value, or N.A.V. Net asset value is the total value of the securities in the fund at the end of each trading day divided by the number of shares outstanding of the fund. That is how you get the cost per share of an open-end mutual fund. So, that even if you buy an open-end mutual in the morning, your broker cannot tell you what you paid for the fund until the next day. Open-end also means the number of shares that can be purchased is unlimited. A closed-end fund is a fund which has a limited number of shares.

An open-end fund and a closed-end fund are similar in that they both have securities in their portfolio, they both charge shareholders for expenses, and they both have N.A.V.'s; however, unlike shares of an open-end fund, shares of a closed-end fund are traded freely in the open market. This means that shares could be bought and sold either below (a discount) or above (a premium) the fund's net asset value. Since the number of shares of a closed-end fund is limited, the price at which you either buy or sell your shares in the open market will depend on the demand for the shares. Clearly, then, there is an additional risk in a closed-end fund. Not only is there fluctuation in net asset value, but also in the demand for the shares, and because of this, there is also an opportunity. If you purchase shares of a closed-end fund whose shares are selling at a significant discount to the net asset value, it is possible in a rising market that not only will the net asset value increase, but the demand for the shares will also increase. This will narrow the discount and possibly put the share price at a premium to net asset value. You can find specific information on closed-end funds in the WALL STREET JOURNAL and BARRONS. They will have the share price, net asset value, and percentage of discount or premium so you can easily be fully informed.

If your broker calls you about a new closed-end fund that is coming to the market, I recommend that you do not purchase it at the initial offering, since the market price is usually at a premium to net asset value. This is due to the fund's initial selling and administrative expenses. As an example, many closed-end funds that came to market in 1988 had an offering price of ten dollars. But the net asset value was $9.30 (usually 7% was expenses). I recommend waiting six months to a year to see how the fund performs, and what the net asset value and demand for the shares are.

One final fact your stockbroker does not want you to know: once the stockbroker purchases the bonds, unit trust, or mutual fund, he has usually already made his commission. Since he cannot make any more commission from these investments, he is usually indifferent about following these investments. Brokers call the money they invested "gone", which means they are unable to generate additional commissions from the money. On mutual funds a broker might make a "trailer commission" from a 12b-1 fee, but this is usually only 10 - 25 basis points per year, very little to give him incentive to follow the performance of the fund. The only way for him to generate additional commissions is for you to sell it and buy something else.

Why invest in mutual funds?

When I ask clients why they invest in mutual funds most of them laugh and say "like everyone else I want to make money". The answer is not as simple as ' I want to make money'. When I ask them to explain why they want their mutual funds to make money their answers differ from person to person. The one answer that was universal was they want to have enough money when they get older. Everyone realized that unless they are financially independent they will not be able to retire.

Most people do not understand that investing money is the same as people working. Here is what I mean. The definition of working is "an occupation in which you get paid a salary or commission". Well, money invested in mutual funds also gets paid. Depending on the type of mutual fund you invest in your money gets paid in three ways: interest income, dividends, or appreciation in value. **Financial independence means having your investments pay you as much as your occupation pays you.** Only then will you be financially secure to retire. The problem is most people have no idea what they need to do today to have financial independence in twenty, thirty, or forty years. It amazes me when I speak to people and they tell me they planned a vacation and they know exactly how much money they will need. Yet when it comes to their retirement they have no idea how to figure it out. I tell them that the same way they have a "Game Plan" for their vacation they need a "Game Plan" for their retirement. A game plan for your retirement is called a "Financial Analysis". Qualified financial professionals have the expertise and software to create a customize financial analysis. Based on the information you give them today they can project what you will need to retire. Remember, this is only a projection. The one thing that is guaranteed is that things change. I suggest you review your financial analysis with your financial professional every year. If your financial situation changes make sure it is updated. This is especially true if the bulk of your money is in an employer sponsored retirement plan. Make sure you contact the plan administrator annually. He will direct you to the financial professional who is there to educate you on your investments.

Update

Since most people complained about the high front end commissions, the brokerage firms have created "B and C'" shares. This is where the client buys the funds at Net Asset Value (NAV) but additional expenses or fees known as "12-b1" fees are added annually. This reduces the annual returns of the fund by usually 1%. Brokers still have to get their commission when the fund is sold. The commission in "B" shares is usually 4% of the investment. If you own "B" shares you have to hold the fund for a period of time before you sell it so you don't get charged a redemption fee. Usually six years. With "C" shares, the broker receives 1% at the time of the sale, and 1% annually as long as you hold the fund.

CHAPTER 4

HOW IMPORTANT
IS THE ACCOUNT FORM?

When you go to a brokerage firm to invest your money, you go with the understanding that the information your stockbroker will provide is accurate and truthful, so that you can make an informed decision on your investments.

Usually, the first time you hear about an investment is either in your stockbroker's office or on the phone with your stockbroker. Since he is the professional on investments you accept his advice. You also assume that what he is doing is in your best interest.

A problem can arise months or sometimes years later when you realize that you were sold an investment that you were unsuited for, or an investment about which you did not understand the risks involved.

If this happens to you, and you and the brokerage firm cannot come to an amicable solution, then arbitration could be your legal remedy.

The arbitration may take place years after the original conversation between you and your stockbroker regarding the investment you purchased. I can almost guarantee you that the stockbroker will remember the conversation differently than you do, thereby making the verbal discussions unreliable and meaningless. That is why the Account Form, usually the only written document the stockbroker has that describes you, becomes so vital in your defense at arbitration.

Thus, the most important and least understood document the stockbroker has a client fill out is the Client Account Form. Every person must fill out an Account Form to receive an account number. This is mandatory before a transaction between you and your stockbroker can occur.

The Client Account Form might look like a basic questionnaire with simple questions, but it is the document that shows if you are suited for certain types of investments. Do not answer these questions lightly or inaccurately. It could cost you dearly in the future.

Before I review the Account Form line by line, I want to emphasize the best advice I can give you. **DON'T EXAGGERATE YOUR EXPERIENCE OR INCOME ON THE ACCOUNT FORM.** If you make $30,000.00 a year, do not state anything higher. When the question is about your investment experience in stocks, bonds, commodities, etc., only put the actual number of years you have been an investor. If you are trying to impress the stockbroker, **DON'T!** Now I will show you how a brokerage firm could interpret your answers on an Account Form. A standard Client Account Form will contain the following questions:

1. **General Information** - name, address, birthdate, social security number, telephone number.
   So far no problem.

2. **Residence** - rent or own. This shows the brokerage firm, right away, that if you own a home, you are not ignorant of all types of investments. Also, if you own a real estate limited partnership you would have some idea of the liquidity and economic risks involved in owning real estate. Thus, if the partnership had decreased in value, you could not claim that you were unaware of the risks in real estate.

3. **Legal residence if different from mailing address** - This shows the brokerage firm if you have more than one home, which is an indication of your assets.

4. **Employment/Job Title/Occupation** - This may show the type of knowledge you might have pertaining to investments in certain industries.

5. **Client state annual income. Client state net worth exclusive of family residence, and estimated liquid net worth** - DO NOT EXAGGERATE. This shows the brokerage firm what portion of your assets is in a specific investment. Having a diversified portfolio of no more than 2-5% of total assets in one investment may not be worth as much

in an arbitration decision as 50% in one investment.

6. **Is the client on a fixed income - Yes or No** - If you are, then say it. By checking this box the stockbroker should be aware that you have no additional income other than your investments, pensions, and/or social security, and that you will probably be a conservative investor.

7. **Is the client an officer, director or 10% stockholder in any corporation** - This tells the brokerage firm that you probably have knowledge about business and investments and also that you have additional assets.

8. **Citizen of U.S.A. (if other please specify)** - If you are not a citizen of the U.S., there may be different tax liabilities depending on your investments and the country that you are from. The stockbroker must be aware of this; otherwise, the brokerage firm, not you, could be liable for any losses incurred.

9. **Former client or account with other brokerage firm** - This shows the brokerage firm the type of investments that you may have made in the past. This will also indicate if you are knowledgeable or suited for certain types of investments.

10. **Investment profile** - Very important! If you want safety of principal and income, **DON'T SAY GROWTH!** Put down only what you want. Also remember, do not put down more investment experience in stock, bonds, options, etc. than what you actually have.

11. **Introduction** - This is where the brokerage firm finds out how you came to open an account. The options are usually seminars, walk/phone in, advertising, personal acquaintance, and referrals. Seminars, personal acquaintances, and referrals may sound innocent, but let me show you what they imply: If you went to a seminar it shows you go out of your way to get knowledge on specific investments. Brokerage firms may say if you have gone to one seminar you may have gone to many and that you are aware of different types of

investments and are probably suited for many investments. If you are referred by a person who is knowledgeable about investments, then there is a good chance you have had discussions about investments, which could imply that you know more about investments than what is stated on the account form. These are possibilities of how a brokerage firm may look at your account form.

12. **References** - name of bank. If you ever have a problem with the brokerage firm they may want to know about your knowledge of investments. References would be a good place to find out this type of information.

13. **Power of attorney** - This means someone besides yourself has the right to handle the money in your account, as well as decide what investments should be made. Be very careful with this, giving someone else this authority may affect your financial situation forever.

14. **Account description** - cash or margin. Cash accounts are the most common. In a cash account, you buy or sell a security (stock, bond, mutual fund, etc.) and pay or receive 100% of the amount, usually within five business days. A Margin Account gives you the right to borrow money on your account (a loan) by using the securities in the account as collateral. For example: If you buy 100 shares of General Electric at $60.00 a share; the total amount you would owe is $6,000.00. In a Margin Account you could borrow up to 50% of the amount owed, which means you would pay $3,000.00 and the brokerage firm would lend you the other $3,000.00 for as long as you keep the General Electric stock in your account. Like any other loan, you will pay interest charges to the brokerage firm for as long as you owe them the $3,000.00. Buying on margin is O.K. **as long as your stockbroker explains, AND YOU UNDERSTAND**, both the risks and the benefits. It is very important to update the account form if your

CHAPTER 5

WHAT YOU SHOULD KNOW
THAT COULD SAVE YOU MONEY

1.   Tell your broker to send you an old copy of the
      Standard and Poors (S & P) book. This monthly
      book gives you the name of issue, ticker symbol,
      rating, principle business, price range, dividend,
      yield, price earnings ratio, financial position,
      capitalization, annual earnings, plus information on
      over 700 mutual funds every month. Most brokers,
      after a month or two, throw out their old copies.
      Most of the information does not change so it is a
      wealth of information that usually ends up in the
      waste basket. If you were to pay for a subscription
      to S & P for a year, you would pay $105.00. So, call
      your broker and save.
      SAVINGS: $105.00

2.   If you are in the market for mutual funds and are
      willing to put in the time and effort, use
      Morningstar.com for your research.
      **Possible savings: hundreds to thousands of
      dollars**

3.   If you decide to buy mutual funds or unit trusts from
      your broker, make sure he tells you about
      BREAKPOINTS.
      SAVINGS: hundred to thousands of dollars.

4.   If you open a margin account at a brokerage firm
      you should understand what you have at risk. What
      you are actually doing is taking out a loan and using
      the securities in your account as collateral. The
      margin rates charged are usually ½% - 2½% over
      the broker loan rate. **MARGIN RATES CAN**

USUALLY BE NEGOTIATED. You can usually negotiate savings of ½% - 1% on the rate.

SAVINGS: **If you margin $25,000.00 you could save $125.00 - $250.00 per year.**

5. **BEWARE!** There are some mutual funds that charge a sales charge on reinvested income. This means that if you reinvest your income by buying more shares in the mutual fund, the fund will charge you an additional sales charge to reinvest. So, if you want to reinvest your income, make sure the fund you decide to buy does not have a sales charge to reinvest.

   SAVINGS: percentage of all reinvested income.

6. If your stockbroker sells you a mutual fund and it **does not perform**, or your investment strategy changes, and your broker tells you to sell the fund and go into another fund, **BEWARE!** Buying a new fund may cost you additional sales charges. Note, however, that exchanging a fund within the same family of funds may cost you very little. Another fund within the same family may meet your investment needs, and to exchange from one fund to another, within the same family, usually has no sales charge or a small administrative fee (five to ten dollars). **DON'T SELL IF YOU CAN EXCHANGE.**

   SAVINGS: Hundreds to thousands of dollars.

7. Make sure every question on the account form is answered accurately. Most people do not answer all the questions, and this could be harmful because it is a document that could help you in the future. For example, if you state on the account form that what you want is steady income and safety of principal, and on the recommendation of your broker, you purchase stock which does not suit you, then the account form can be used to illustrate your investment goals. Your broker should have realized

from the account form that you may have been unsuited for that particular type of investment. **SAVINGS: A lot of aggravation and possibly money.**

8. **BEWARE!** Many stockbrokers after you explain your needs may recommend what is known as a proprietary product. This could be a mutual fund, or other product, that is sold by the brokerage firm salesman, as well as managed by the brokerage firm itself. Such products enable the firm to make both a commission from selling it, and a continuing fee from managing it. As a result, the firm gives the salesman an incentive to sell these products rather than other products. The incentive may be in the form of higher payouts of commission or special gifts if they sell a certain amount. Before you buy any proprietary product, ask your salesman to show you its track record (performance record) for the past one, three, five, and ten years, if possible. You should then compare it to other investments in the same category, and this way you can judge if your salesman's recommendation is truly in your best interest.

9. Clients often ask if the sales load charged when they bought a mutual fund is tax deductible as an expense. The answer is that it usually is not, but there is a strategy. What you can do is to buy a fund in a family of funds which allows switching from one fund to another. Switching is actually a buy and a sell. If you invest $10,000.00 in a fund with a six percent sales load, the net asset value (N.A.V.) is actually only $9,400.00. If you wait a month and then switch to the fund you actually want, you will switch at N.A.V., which, depending on the N.A.V. at that time could give you a short term loss. Because the government changes the tax laws so often, you should call your accountant to see if this is still possible; if it is, you may be able to save a lot of

money.

10.   The best way to save money is to know exactly what you need to achieve financial freedom. The way to do this is to have a professional financial analysis. A financial analysis is an examination or review of all your assets and liabilities. This review, usually done by a financial professional, includes all your incomes, investments, homes, mortgages, insurance, credit cards, loans, etc. A good financial analysis will give you a "Game Plan" on how to attain your financial goal. Many companies offer financial analysis. A financial analysis will cost between a few hundred dollars to as high as a few thousand dollars. One company, **Primerica Financial Services**, which is a division of **Citigroup**, offers the best value for a professional financial analysis. Primerica, which creates a custom design financial report, does not charge a monetary fee for this service. Their marketing approach is, if you are satisfied with the service provided in the creation of their financial analysis, they ask for referrals as their fee.

CHAPTER 6

ARBITRATION

Many customers who have had claims against brokerage firms have won financial awards. In 2001, there were more than 6900 arbitration cases filed. Cases where customers received awards decided by arbitrators was 53%.

In 2002, the results were even better. There were over 7700 cases filed for arbitration. Cases where customers received awards decided by arbitrators were 55%. This does not include all the cases that are settled prior to the arbitration panel making a decision. Almost 50% of the arbitration cases are settled before a decision is made. This means 75%, or three out of four people who file for arbitration get back part or all of their money.

Here is a list of terms that you should know since they are the most common reasons for customer complaints in arbitration cases.

1. **Churning** - This is where the stockbroker excessively buys and sells in an account specifically to generate commissions. It is illegal for the broker to generate trades, or churn, a client's account. Churning can usually be proven in two ways. The first is known as the "Looper Method" or turnover ratio. An example of this would be if your opening balance in your account is $100,000 and the purchases of securities in the account is $600,000, then the turnover ratio is 6:1. The next method is known as the "Goldberg Cost / Equity Maintenance Factor". This is simply determining the

client's costs, or commission, of the trades. As an example, if you do ten round trip trades in a year and each buy and sell has a total commission of 3%, you need to make at least 30% on all the trades in your account just to cover costs.

2. **Misrepresentation** - This is when a broker **intentionally** omits important facts or misleads you on the risks of certain investments. Example: a government mutual fund does not mean the government guarantees payments made by the mutual fund. So, if the broker says it's "government guaranteed" he is misrepresenting the mutual fund.

3. **Unsuitability** - This is when your investments do not meet your investment profile. If your investment profile states that you want safety of principal and conservative income, then you may be unsuited for high risk investments; i.e., certain types of option and speculative stocks and bonds. You may also be financially unsuitable for a specific investment.

4. **Unauthorized Trading** - This is when a broker trades (buy or sell) in an account without the customer giving the broker authority.

5. **Negligence** - This is when a broker or firm does not act in the customer's best interest. This could be done by not following a customer's order or omitting pertinent information on an investment.

If you have a complaint against your brokerage firm or stockbroker, the first step is to contact the branch manager as soon as possible. You should do this in writing. If you are not satisfied with the results, you should contact, in writing, the president of the brokerage firm. Again, if you are not satisfied, then your options are mediation, arbitration, or possibly, litigation. What a mediator tries to do is to bring both sides together to discuss the case and how it might be settled. Any decision made by the mediator is **NOT** binding on either party. It is only a suggestion.

Arbitration is a legal means of resolving disputes; it is binding on both parties. It is important to know that you do not need an attorney to go to arbitration. You should, however, consider at least consulting an attorney in order to find out what to expect in an arbitration hearing. If you decide to go for a consultation, look for an attorney who has arbitration experience and is familiar with securities law. If you feel you need an attorney, try to find one who will accept your case on a contingency fee basis, so that if you do not prevail and no award is granted to you, then you will only be responsible for the costs of the arbitration, and not your attorney's fees. If you want to know more about the costs and procedures of arbitration, contact the National Association of Securities Dealers (N.A.S.D.) at:

N.A.S.D. Financial Center
One Liberty Plaza
New York, New York 10006
Tel # 212-858-4000

This organization will have virtually all the information you will need, and will send it to you.

Update

Before you go to arbitration there is an additional forum in the securities industry known as Mediation. In contrast to arbitration, mediation tries to get both sides to settle the dispute with an acceptable compromise to both parties. Mediators are neutrals. They don't make any decisions or awards. It is also an informal process. The costs are less than an arbitration.

CHAPTER 7

PREPARING FOR AN
ARBITRATION

If you have tried to work out an agreement with the brokerage firm over your losses but were unsuccessful and feel you have exhausted all alternatives, then you must prepare to file for arbitration. Begin with gathering all documents that relate to your account and your claim and put them in chronological order. Start from the beginning, which will probably be the opening account forms including the customer agreements. If you do not have these documents, write a letter to the branch manager of the local office and ask him to send it to you within 10 days. Do not just call on the phone, follow up with letters every week until you receive them. Go over each question on the account form: note what type of account you had - cash or margin; do you have more than one account at the brokerage firm; what investment objective was checked off; did you check them off or did the broker; was your background information completed; did you complete it or did the broker; is your birth date correct; is your prior investment history, income and net worth correct as of the time the account was opened; did you sign the account form after you answered all of the questions; did you complete the account form at home or in the broker's office; do you remember why you opened an account at that particular brokerage firm and why you chose that particular broker; did you give the broker discretion over your account - that is, did the broker initiate the trades in your account; and did you give him written authority to do so?

Next, put together all the monthly statements and

trade confirmations in chronological order. Note any trades in question. Here is some advice - don't write anything on the original statements or confirmations as you will probably have to produce them for the respondents or brokerage firm. They may get additional information from these comments that you don't want them to have. Also these comments might affect your credibility to the arbitration panel.

Next, check the gross commissions on the confirmations, if you feel they were excessive, add them up by month and in total. You should understand that some confirmations will show no commissions. This happens when the brokerage firm acts as principal or market maker in a specific security. Ask the brokerage firm what profit they made on these trades. If they don't tell you, you will get it later when you ask the firm for the "commission run" of the broker. This is a monthly statement showing how much commission the broker made on each trade.

Next, put together any correspondence you had with the broker. Did he send you any information on specific products, research reports, prospectuses or recommendations on a specific security you invested in? Did you ever write letters to the broker or branch manager complaining about a specific investment? Did they respond in writing? After you have gathered all this information, write a detailed account of what happened to you. Use documents to verify your statements. Start from the beginning when you opened the account and put in as much detail as possible. One more thing, if there is an individual who can help you verify any information about the claim, make sure you put them in the statement. Example, were you with your spouse or a friend when you opened the account or when you and the broker had a discussion on the specific investment in question? Did your accountant ever speak to your broker? Did you ever speak to the branch manager? What was the conversation?

At this point, you may or may not decide to use an attorney. If you decide to use an attorney, your next question is how do you find one? Here are a few suggestions: First, referral from friends, acquaintances, accountants or other professional people. They may know an attorney who specializes in securities and arbitration law. Second, call the local bar association for a list of attorneys specializing in this type of law. Choose one or two and call them for a consultation. At this stage, it is worth paying for their time to find one you are comfortable with. Usually, they won't charge you for the initial consultation. If, after you discuss your case, the attorney does not accept you as a client, ask him why. If he feels you do not have a good case, you may reconsider the claim. If he accepts you as a client, find out how he charges for his services. If it is an hourly charge, get a rough estimate of what that could be. The charge would vary greatly, depending on if the case is settled early on before arbitration or if you have to go through the entire arbitration process. His fee may be on a contingent fee basis. This means he will receive a percentage of the financial award, if he wins an award. Most attorneys will ask for a retainer. This will usually be a few thousand dollars. Make sure you ask what expenses are and are not covered by the retainer.

If you decide not to use an attorney, your next step is to obtain and fill out the filing forms for the arbitration. You should also receive the rules or Code of Arbitration Procedure. This booklet will tell you the costs involved to file, plus other pertinent information. The first form you will fill out is the Statement of Claim - your name, the brokerage firm's name, the dollar amount in dispute and the relief requested, issues to be determined by the arbitrators - in other words, your side of the story. Be specific, put in as much detail in chronological order and copies of documents to verify your claim against the brokerage firm and the broker. Show as strong as possible why they should be responsible and not you for your losses. Also put in the total amount of damages you request, such as attorneys' fees or punitive damages. Remember, you have to prove to the arbitrators that you are right and the brokerage firm was wrong. Also, don't grossly overstate your damages. You filing fees are based on damages claimed and your credibility may be affected if you overly exaggerate your damages. You will I also fill out a cover sheet for your statement of claim that will only be used by the forum staff.

ARBITRATORS

If you have a panel of three arbitrators, one will be affiliated with the securities industry. The other two will be public arbitrators from outside the securities industry. You will be entitled to the names and employment histories of the arbitrators, plus you may request copies of all awards rendered in previous arbitrations by these arbitrators. This could show a preference or a conflict of interest of a specific arbitrator. If you object to a specific arbitrator for good cause, they will probably be replaced.

Once you file the Statement of Claim and the brokerage firm answers the claim, you may want additional documents from the brokerage firm. Make sure your request is in writing. Request the following documents (even if you already have them):

(1)   **Opening account forms.**

(2)   **Customer agreements.**

(3)   **Option agreements.**

(4)   **Margin agreements.**

(5)   **Any and all documents you have ever signed.** These documents usually will show suitability for and your awareness of specific investments.

(6)   **Monthly account statements and confirmations.** These documents will show trading activity in the account. This could be important if the claim is for suitability, churning or unauthorized trading.

(7)   **The brokerage firm's compliance manuals and/or account executive manuals.** This can be useful if the broker did not follow specific standards that are required by the brokerage firm. Also may show that the firm did not adequately supervise the account executive.

(8)   **Forms U-4 and U-5.** The U-4 is filled out by the broker when he is hired by the firm. This form will show any disciplinary history or claims filed against the account executive. The U-5 is filled out and gives the reasons why and when the broker leaves the firm. Was it voluntary or involuntary? Also try to get the U-5 from the broker's previous firms.

(9) **Due diligence reports.** This is information the brokerage firm puts together after researching facts on a specific company or product that they recommend. These facts may prove stability, untrue statements, or misrepresentations made by the broker for you to invest in this product.

(10) **Prospectuses and sales literature.** This could show suitability for a recommended investment by the broker, also possible omission of facts and misrepresentations.

(11) **Account executive holding page and order tickets.** The holding page shows the activity of the account by the broker. This could be used to show churning, unauthorized trading or failure to supervise. Order tickets show the exact time the order was put in to be executed. You might prove the broker called you in the afternoon, convinced and recommended that you buy a specific investment when he actually bought it for you in the morning.

(12) **Commission runs for your account.** This could show excessive commissions charged to your account.

You should also remember that the brokerage firm has the right to request documents from you to prove their case. Brokerage firms do not want to give you back money. They are going to do whatever is necessary to prove you were knowledgeable about the investment. Here is a list of typical documents requested by brokerage firms:

(1) **Federal and other income tax returns.** This could help them in knowing your financial status.

(2) **Loan applications.** This could show financial ability and financial history.

(3) **Any correspondence the brokerage firm sent you.** These documents could show your awareness of certain investments and activity.

(4) **Other brokerage firm's account applications and activities.** These will show what type of information and trading activity you are doing at another firm.

(5) **Your resume.** This will show education, business experience, and memberships to organizations or clubs. This could show the type of sophistication and knowledge on certain investments.

(6) **Lists of subscriptions to publications, newsletters and clubs.** This could show knowledge to certain investments. Another fact you should know is that there are public sources where you can obtain information on brokerage firm's personnel, the branch manager and the broker. The main source is the **Central Registration Depository (CRD).** You may obtain any disciplinary records, awards or settlements by brokerage firms or their brokers, plus biographical and licensing data. The telephone number is (301) 590-6500. If you care to write to them, their address is: NASD/CRD, 9513 Key West Avenue, Rockville, Maryland 20850.

After you have prepared the next step is the hearing. The chairperson will formally open the hearing and administer an oath to all parties and witnesses. You will have your opening statement. This will be what you intend to prove. This should be concise and well planned. The respondent will do the same. Then you will present your case. The opposing side has the right to object to your documents and evidence.

At that point, the arbitrators will ask why they are objecting to your evidence. After the explanation, the panel may accept or reject the objection. If you have a witness to help your case, the respondents have a right to cross-examine them. The respondents will try to reduce the damage his testimony has brought or they may try to damage his credibility. When you finish your presentation of your allegations, documents and witnesses, the respondent will present its case. Remember, you also have the right to object to their evidence and witnesses. You also have the right to cross-examine their witnesses. When the respondent finishes its case, the panel has a right to ask additional questions of either party or witnesses. If there are no more questions or witnesses, then both parties are allowed closing arguments. Your closing argument should show what you believe your evidence and witnesses have proved and what the respondent's evidence and witnesses failed to prove against you. The arbitrators will try to render a decision for an award within thirty (30) days. You may or may not win and the arbitrators do not have to give a reason for their decision.

Update

When preparing for an arbitration go to www.nasdadr.com. You will be able to get all the forms. You can also get different arbitration cases that could relate to your case to review. You can also get the brokers U4. This will give you past and present information on the broker.

CHAPTER 8

DID YOU BUY MUTUAL FUNDS?

Between 1984 and 2000 the brokerage firm industry received enormous revenue for selling specific types of mutual funds. Billions of dollars of these funds were sold to the public.

Many of these funds have gone down in value. A lot of people got angry, and some even took the brokerage firms to arbitration to get their money back. Many people felt the volatility of the fund was either misrepresented to them or that their broker should have realized that they were unsuited for this type of investment.

The next pages show the decisions of arbitration cases when mutual funds were either a cause or part of the cause for the arbitration. These decisions are presented with a case summary, the relief requested, and the award granted. I have used initials instead of the actual names of the claimants, in order to protect their privacy. Since decisions and awards were not made public prior to May, 1989, there are only a small number of cases available where arbitrators made a financial award to customers. Remember that as many as 50% of all cases between customers and brokerage firms are settled before the arbitrator makes a final decision. It should also be understood that just because one arbitration panel agrees with a customer in a specific action on a specific product, **THIS IS NOT A GUARANTEE OR PRECEDENT ON ANY OTHER ARBITRATION.** Arbitrators base their decision on the facts and merits of each case, not on other arbitration cases. At the end of the case I've noted the reason why the claimant filed for arbitration and any important facts about the awards.

CHAPTER 9

ARBITRATION AWARDS - MUTUAL FUNDS

Number: 1101   MF Van Wagoner Mid-Cap Fund

Claimant: B.W.F.

Respondent: Prudential Securities

CASE SUMMARY

This claim was filed on or about December 2000.

Claimant asserted the following causes of action: breach of contract, negligence, and failure to execute, and breach of fiduciary duty. Respondents denied the allegations made in the Statement of Claim. Respondent states that all times claimant had or should have had full knowledge of all material facts concerning the investment he made, including the nature of the investments and the associated risks. Claimant directed and authorized the execution of all transactions in his account. Respondents are not liable for losses because they were within the risks
Claimant chose to assume.

RELIEF REQUESTED

Claimant requested compensatory damages in the amount of $ 17,980.12 plus punitive damages, interest at the rate of 12%, attorney's fees, and forum fees.

AWARD

Prudential is solely liable for and shall pay the Claimant the sum of $10,077.20 as compensatory damages, plus interest at 12% per annum from December 21, 2000 totaling $1,612.32, for a total award of $11,689.52

DATE AND PLACE

April 11, 2001 Boston, Massachusetts

Note: Even though the Claimant should have known the risks and did authorize the transactions, the arbitration panel still found Prudential liable.

Number: 1012

Claimant: HD

Respondent: Prudential Securities

CASE SUMMARY
The case was filed July 31, 2001.
Claimant alleges unsuitable investments in aggressive stocks, all Internet and telecommunications related, misrepresentation, Violation of Florida State Statutes, breach of contract, negligence and failure to supervise.

RELIEF REQUESTED
Claimant requested $280.000.

AWARD
The respondent shall pay to the claimant the sum of $257,251.45, $256,501.45 as an award on the claim and $750.00 as a return of claimant's deposit of costs. The claimant prevailed on the claim under Florida Statute 517.301 and is therefore entitled to attorney's fee.

DATE AND PLACE
April 18, 2002 Fort Lauderdale, Florida

Note: Claimant was unsuitable for internet and telecommunication investments. Also claimant received his attorney's fees back.

Number: 1103

Claimant: EJC & HBC

Respondent: Merrill Lynch

CASE SUMMARY
The case was filed February 5, 2002.
Claimant alleged that the respondent purchased stock that was unsuitable for their age and investment objectives. Claimant maintains that due to respondent's action, the account suffered losses.

RELIEF REQUESTED
Claimant is asking for $25,000.00

AWARD
Respondent is liable and shall pay the Claimant $25,000.00.

DATE AND PLACE
August 12, 2002, Newport Beach, California

Note: What is important about this case is that first the claimants appeared pro se, which means they did it themselves without an attorney. Also they got back 100% of what they asked for. These investments were unsuitable for their age and investment objective.

Number: 1130

Claimant: JB

Respondent: Salomon Smith Barney

CASE SUMMARY
The case was filed November 5, 2001.
The claimant alleges that the registered representative made unauthorized trades in the account and that the account incurred substantial charges from the sale of mutual funds.

RELIEF REQUESTED
Claimant requested $6,248.00

AWARD
Salomon Smith Barney shall pay JB $1,454.00 as an award on the Statement of Claim. Forum fees are assessed against the Respondent.

DATE AND PLACE
April 19, 2002 Philadelphia, PA.

Number: 103MF   E.F. Hutton
                                         Improperly switching funds
Claimants: L.M. and J.M.

Respondent: E.F. Hutton & Company, Inc. and J.Sm.

AWARD

1. Respondents E.F. Hutton & Company, Inc. and J.S. are jointly and severally liable for and shall pay to the Claimants the sum of Seven Thousand, Nine Hundred, Eight-Four Dollars and Four Cents ($7,984.04) which represents commissions charged by Respondent for improperly switching Claimants' funds from the Putnam Hi Income Government Trust to the Hutton Government Securities Series, a change which did not result in significant or material benefit to Claimants.

2. Respondents E.F. Hutton & Company, Inc. and J.S. are jointly and severally liable for and shall pay to the Claimants the sum of $400.00 (Four Hundred Dollars and Zero Cents) representing payment of the filing fee previously deposited with the National Association of Securities Dealers, Inc. by Claimant.

DATE

December 8, 1988

NOTE: Stockbroker switching a client from one load fund to another load fund without reasonable benefit to the client.

Number: 104MF

Piper, Jaffray
Keystone Tax Free Fund

Claimants: R. & D. T.

Respondents: Piper, Jaffray & Hopwood, Inc. and S.F.

SUMMARY OF ISSUES

This case was filed on September 20, 1988. Claimant's Alleged misrepresentation in the purchase of shares of a mutual fund, Keystone Tax Free Fund. Respondents denied the allegations of Claimants and alleged the following affirmative defenses: claims barred by the applicable statutes of limitation; laches; failure to state a claim upon which relief can be granted; respondents acted in good faith; damages allegedly suffered have no causal relationship with any act or omission attributable to respondents; failure to mitigate damages; claimants did not reasonable rely on any act or omission of respondents; waiver.

DAMAGES AND RELIEF REQUESTED

Claimants requested compensatory damages of $7,215.56. Respondents requested costs and disbursements.

DAMAGES AND RELIEF AWARDED

1. Respondents are jointly and severally liable for and shall pay to claimants the sum of $5,772.45 in compensatory damages.
2. The parties shall each bear their respective costs including attorneys' fees.

NOTE: Misrepresented facts about a mutual fund. What is important about this case is the broker says the client waited too long to file the claim.

Number: 105MF

Claimants: I. & M. N.

Respondents: Comm Vest Securities, Inc.

CASE SUMMARY
This claim was filed with the NASD, Inc. on May 26, 1989. The hearing was conducted in Fort Lauderdale, Florida on February 13, 1990 with a total of one (1) session.

Claimants, I. and M. N. ("N"), alleged that Respondent, CommVest Securities, Inc. ("CommVest"), recommended the purchase of Putnam High Income Government Trust as a "no risk" safe investment, to preserve principal, earn 12% interest and quarterly dividend checks; that through its broker, R. M., CommVest made misrepresentations of material facts and omitted to state material facts; and, used high pressure to sell Claimants on unsuitable investment. Respondent denied all allegations of wrongdoing; alleged that it fully and truthfully advised the Claimants about the Putnam investment from the Putnam documents; that the investment appeared to be suitable in providing a stable income for retirees; that Putnam's own mismanagement may have caused the demise of the fund; that Claimants are not novice investors and made a voluntary and informed purchase of the fund at issue.

RELIEF REQUESTED
Claimants requested damages in the amount of $50,000.00 for the value their investment would have been worth today (principal plus interest). Respondent requested dismissal of the claim and an award in favor of CommVest.

AWARD
1. Respondent, CommVest, is hereby liable and shall pay to Claimants the amount of Eleven Thousand and 00/100 ($11,000.00) Dollars inclusive of interest.

DATE
February 13, 1990

NOTE: Misrepresented and omitted facts about government fund. What is important about case is that the brokerage firm tries to put the blame on the fund's management itself. Also brokerage firm says client was

71

knowledgeable investor and should have known the risks.

Number: 108MF   Volatility of Franklin Fund

Claimants: W. & D. J.

Respondents: McLaughlin, Piven, Vogel, Inc.

CASE SUMMARY
Date filed: 7/21/89
First scheduled: 12/13/89
Decided: 12/13/89.
Customer alleges that they were misinformed regarding the volatility of
the Franklin Fund.

RELIEF REQUESTED
$1,300.00

AWARD
$1,000.00
The Claimant is to receive from Respondent $1,025.00. $1,000.00
representing the award, and $25.00 representing the costs assessed.
Costs are assessed against the Respondent.

DATE AND PLACE
December 13, 1989 in New York City, NY

NOTE: Broker misinformed them of the volatility. Also it was worth
going to arbitration for as little as $1300.00.

Claimant: D. E.

Respondent: Shearson Lehman Hutton, Inc. and D. B.

CASE SUMMARY
Customer vs. member firm and registered representative. Claimant alleges she is ill and invested $125,000.00 in Hutton Investment Securities to meet her stated investment objectives of preservation of principal and a 12% return. Claimant further alleges that her broker highly recommended that she transfer her funds to
the Colonial Tax Exempt High Yield Fund which resulted in a penalty.

AWARD REQUESTED
$10,624.00

AWARD
$9,502.92
The Respondents, Shearson Lehman Hutton, Inc, and D. B., are hereby jointly and severally liable to pay to the Claimant the sum of $9,902.92, representing an award on the claim in the amount of $9,502.92, and a return of Claimant's deposit of costs of $400.00. The claim was originally scheduled for a hearing. However, due to Claimant's illness the parties agreed to submit the matter for a determination based on the pleadings.

DATE AND PLACE
December 8, 1989 in New York City, NY

NOTE: Switching from one load fund to another load fund without reasonable benefit to client.

Number: 111MF

Merrill Lynch,
Pierce, Fenner & Smith

Claimant: W. R. and B. R.

Unauthorized trades

Respondents: Merrill Lynch, Pierce, Fenner & Smith, Inc. and R. B.

CASE SUMMARY

This claim was filed with the NASD, Inc. on June 16, 1988. The hearing was conducted in Tampa, Florida on August 15, 1989 and September 19, 1989 with a total of six (6) sessions.

Claimants W. R. and B. R. ("the R's) alleged that Respondents Merrill Lynch, Pierce, Fenner & Smith, Inc. ("Merrill") and R. B. ("B"): failed to follow the trading instructions of the Claimants; executed unauthorized trades in Claimants' account and engaged in a fraudulent course of conduct to conceal Respondents' failure to follow trading instructions and the unauthorized trades. Respondents denied liability and alleged that: the losses suffered were beyond Respondents' control; Claimants either authorized or ratified all trades; Claimants have waived or are estopped from claiming unauthorized trades and Claimants actual losses were less than those asked for in the Statement of Claim.

RELIEF REQUESTED

Claimants requested damages in the amount of $167,943.31 plus interest, punitive damages, attorney's fees and other costs. Respondents requested dismissal of the claim and other costs.

AWARD

1. Respondent Merrill is hereby liable and shall pay to Claimants the following amounts:

a. For Respondent Merrill's failure to sell Claimants' ML Eurofund mutual fund on October 16, 1987, the sum of Forty Seven Thousand Seventy and 31/100 ($47,070.31) Dollars plus interest at the legal rate of 12% per annum from October 16, 1987 to the date of payment of this Award.

b. For Respondent Merrill's failure to sell Claimants' ML Natural Resources Trust mutual fund on October 9, 1987, the sum of Nine Thousand Two Hundred Seventy-Five and 42/100 ($9,275.42) Dollars plus interest at the legal rate of 12% per annum from October 9, 1987 to the date of payment of this Award.

74

2. Respondent Merrill is hereby liable and shall, to the extent it has not already done so, credit Claimants' account: Four Thousand Five Hundred Fifty and 40/100 ($4,550.40) Dollars for the Capital Fund mutual fund; Four Thousand Two Hundred Eighty-Six and 59/100 ($4,286.59) Dollars for the International Holdings mutual fund; and Four Thousand Six Hundred Twelve and 50/100 ($4,612.50) Dollars for the Basic Value mutual fund.

DATE

February 16, 1990

NOTE: Broker failed to follow client's instruction and did unauthorized trade in accounts.

Claimant: H. F.

Respondents: Easter Kramer Group Securities, Inc. and C. H.

CASE SUMMARY

This claim was filed with the NASD, Inc. on September 26, 1988. The hearing was conducted in Fort Lauderdale, Florida on October 17, 1989 with a total of two (2) sessions. The Claimant, H. F. ("F") alleged that Respondent, Easter Kramer Group Securities, Inc. ("Easter Kramer") and C. H. were liable for damages sustained by: Respondents' failure to inform Claimant of a price break and letter of intent which he was entitled to: failure to provide Claimant with a switch letter that would have advised him that he would have to pay a further commission when he switched the funds and failure to inform Claimant of the disadvantages of buying different families of funds. Also, claimant alleged: that the second switch was into an unsuitable fund and that Respondents were liable for fraud and negligence. Respondents asserted the affirmative defenses of: good faith; waiver; estoppel; laches and lack of proximate cause. Additionally, Respondents alleged that: Claimant had failed to set forth allegations to support an award of punitive damages; H acted in compliance with all applicable rules and regulations; Respondents were not negligent or reckless and Claimant never informed Respondents that he would be investing over $100,000.00 which would have entitled him to the price break.

AWARD

D. E., representative of Easter Kramer, told staff attorney, A. F. on October 16, 1989 via telephone, that he did not plan on attending the hearing and that; therefore, Easter Kramer would not have a representative there.

1. Respondents are hereby liable, jointly and severally, and shall pay to Claimant the amount of One Thousand Three Hundred Five and 76/100 ($1,305.76) Dollars inclusive of interest at the legal rate of 12% per annum.

DATE

October 17, 1989

NOTE: Breakpoints. It is also important when switching from one fund to another. Client must be told of the cost. This is done by a switch letter.

Number: 116MF   Shearson Lehman
                                            Sophisticated Investor
Claimant: A & R K

Respondents: Shearson Lehman Brothers, Inc. and E. F.

CASE SUMMARY
In a claim filed with the National Association of Securities Dealers, Inc. on June 6, 1988, Claimant A & R K Realty alleged the Respondents misrepresented the yield the Claimant would receive on its investment in the Shearson Lehman Brothers, Inc. Special Tax Exempt Income Portfolio and told the Claimant the investment would provide complete portfolio liquidity and misrepresented to the Claimant that the investment did not contain any fees for redemption upon liquidation of the fund. Respondents Shearson Lehman Brothers, Inc. and E. F. maintained they never "guaranteed" a fixed yield to the Claimant and the Claimant as an experienced and ultra sophisticated investor knew no guarantee existed and further maintained Respondents never represented to the Claimant that there were no redemption fees upon liquidation. Respondents Shearson Lehman Brothers, Inc. and E. F. further maintained any losses incurred were the result of Claimant's own deliberate and informed investment decisions.

RELIEF REQUESTED
Claimant requested damages of $37,000.00. Respondents requested dismissal of claim plus costs.

AWARD
The Respondent Shearson Lehman Bothers, Inc. be and hereby is liable and shall pay to the claimant A & R K the sum of Twenty Four Thousand Dollars and No Cents ($24,000.00), inclusive of interest.

DATE AND PLACE
March 14, 1990 in New York City, New York

NOTE: Misrepresentation. Also Shearson says claimant was "experienced and ultra sophisticated" investor.

Number: 125MF

Prudential
Unsuitable Funds

Claimants: S. & L. P.

Respondents: Prudential-Bache Securities, Inc., Pruco Securities Corp.,
T. N., D. R., L. G., Prudential Insurance Company of America

CASE SUMMARY

Claimants alleged that Respondents misrepresented investments when
advising Claimants to move monies from their IRA accounts at another
institution to accounts governed by the Respondents. Claimants further
alleged that Respondents placed them in unsuitable funds and failed to
disclose the facts of and misrepresented insurance policies that were
sold to them where the principals were at risk. Respondents Pruco
Securities Corp., T. N., L. G. and D. R. maintained that prospectuses
were provided to the Claimants and that no guarantees were ever made
to the Claimants who signed applications verifying that the contract met
their financial needs and objectives. Respondent Prudential-Bache
Securities maintained that they were not a proper party to the
proceeding. Respondent Prudential Insurance Company of America
requested that they be dismissed as a party and asserted that they were
not a proper respondent to the complaint.

AWARD

1. The Motion to Dismiss of Prudential Insurance Company to dismiss
   the firm as party is denied.
2. As decided by this panel at the hearing on November 14, 1989, the
   Motion to Dismiss of Prudential-Bache Securities, Inc. to dismiss
   Prudential-Bache Securities, Inc. as a party to this proceeding is
   granted.
3. Pruco Securities Corp., Prudential Insurance Company of American
   and D. R. shall be jointly and severally liable and shall pay to the
   Claimants the sum of Eleven Thousand Six Hundred Eighty
   Dollars and Seventy-Five Cents ($11,680.75) inclusive of interest.
4. The claims of the Claimants against T. N. and L. G. are hereby
   dismissed.

DATE AND PLACE

November 14, 1989 in Buffalo, New York

NOTE: Misrepresented investments, suitability.

Number: 122MF

Claimant: D. & L. S.

Prudential
Failure to Follow Instruction

Respondents: Prudential-Bache Securities, Inc. and J. K.

CASE SUMMARY

Date filed: 12/31/88
First scheduled: 9/19/90
Decided: 1/12/90

Claimants allege they retained Respondent broker to rollover a retirement fund containing 1951 shares of Tucson Electric Power Stock. Claimants further allege Respondent did successfully rollover two funds (Washington Mutual and American Capital) but failed to rollover a third fund, Massachusetts Financial.

RELIEF REQUESTED

$29,000.00

AWARD

$24,800.00

The Respondent, Prudential-Bache Securities, Inc. shall pay to the Claimants the sum of $24,800.00, representing an award on the claim inclusive of attorney's fees and interest; the costs, $800.00, be and hereby are assessed against the Respondent, Prudential-Bache Securities, Inc.

DATE AND PLACE

January 12, 1990 in Phoenix, Arizona

NOTE: Failure of broker to follow instructions.

Number: 126MF

Merrill Lynch
Misrepresentation

Claimant: T. S.

Respondents: Merrill Lynch, Pierce, Fenner & Smith, Inc., and M. L.

CASE SUMMARY

Claimant T. S. alleged that he wanted to open an IRA account with the Respondent Merrill Lynch, Pierce, Fenner & Smith, Inc., namely the Merrill Lynch Federal Securities Trust Fund. Claimant alleged that Respondent M. L. guaranteed that no commissions would be charged on the purchase of this Fund. Claimant further alleged that Respondent L. never purchased this Fund for his account, but instead purchased the Merrill Lynch Retirement Income Fund. Claimant alleged he then informed Respondent L. to close the Fund and return his monies, for which the Claimant was charged a commission. Claimant also alleged that he purchased shares in the Merrill Lynch Hubbard Income Realty Partnership VI, and was assured by Respondent L. of the investment's complete liquidity. Claimant alleged he ordered the sale of this investment, and that the Respondents to date have not done so. Respondents Merrill Lynch and M. L. denied any and all allegations of wrongdoing or liability in the Claimant's claim for damages. Respondents maintained the Claimant was fully informed that a commission would be charged on the purchase of the Federal Securities Trust Fund, and that Respondent L. purchased the Retirement Income Fund for Claimant instead because he knew of claimant's desire to avoid commissions. Moreover, Respondents contended the Claimant received a prospectus on the Merrill Lynch Hubbard Income Realty Partnership VI, and was fully apprised of the risks involved with this investment. Respondents further contended that they acted properly and that the Claimant authorized all trades.

RELIEF REQUESTED

Claimant T. S. requested that his Merrill Lynch Hubbard Income Realty Partnership VI fund be closed and his $2,000.00 investment returned to him, plus $454.97 in damages. Respondents Merrill Lynch, Pierce, Fenner & Smith, Inc. and M. L. requested dismissal of the claim in its entirety, plus costs.

AWARD

1. Because this panel is convinced by the testimony of Mr. S. and Mr.

L. that Mr. S. never understood the particulars of the investments which Mr. L. proposed to sell him, the panel finds that:

a. Claimant T. S. is entitled to the rescission of his Two Thousand Dollars and No Cents ($2,000.00) investment in the Merrill Lynch Hubbard Income Realty Partnership VI, and Respondent Merrill Lynch, Pierce, Fenner & Smith, Inc. be and hereby is ordered and directed to take whatever steps are necessary to extract Mr. S. from this partnership, and to pay to him forthwith the sum of Two Thousand Dollars and No Cents ($2,000.00), without interest.

b. Respondent Merrill Lynch, Pierce, Fenner & Smith, Inc. be and hereby is liable and shall pay to the Claimant Three Hundred and Eighty-Three Dollars and Eighty Two Cents ($383.82).

2. All claims against Respondent M. L. be and hereby are dismissed in their entirety.

3. The parties each shall bear their respective costs including attorney's fees.

DATE AND PLACE
December 14, 1989 in New York City, New York

NOTE: Misrepresented fees and negligence about other facts. Arbitrators convinced claimant never understood investment.

Number: 133MF

Claimant: G. A. et. al.

Respondent: Merrill Lynch and P. L.

CASE SUMMARY
Date filed: 9/29/88
FIRST scheduled: 11/14/89
Decided: 2/13/90
Claimants' assert Respondents failed to adequately advise Claimants that the exchange of one bond fund for another would result in realized capital tax losses.

AWARD
Award: $4,500.00
Punitive: None
Atty fees: None
Costs: $750.00
Claimant shall receive $4,500.00 from Merrill Lynch. Each party shall be responsible for their own Attorney's fees and costs.

DATE AND PLACE
February 13, 1990 in Miami, Florida

NOTE: Failure to advise client switching within a family of funds is actually a buy and sell, which could realize a capital tax gain or loss.

Number: 135MF

A.G Edwards
Risks of a Margin Account

Claimant: K. R.

Respondent: A.G. Edwards & Sons, Inc. and E. M.

CASE SUMMARY

K. B. ("Claimant") alleged as follows:

1. E. M. ("M"), a registered representative of A. G. Edwards & Sons, Inc., (E. M. and A. G. Edwards are collectively referred to herein as "Respondents") acted as the Claimant's representative during the time period of June 16, 1982 through September 17, 1985 and engaged in the following acts or omissions:

    a. Churned the Claimant's account;

    b. Purchased unsuitable securities for the Claimant;

    c. Placed the Claimant on margin without her authorization; such margin account was unsuitable for Claimant, M. did not explain to the Claimant the risk of trading on margin; and a margin account was established for the purpose of generating more commissions;

    d. Switched the Claimant's mutual funds for other mutual funds and stock for the purpose of generating commissions;

    e. Made trades in the Claimant's account without the Claimant's authorization;

    f. Wrongfully guaranteed the price of Phibro Salomon stock.

2. A. G. Edwards failed to properly supervise M.

3. Respondent improperly by executed an option trade without securing the necessary documentation.

4. The above acts and omissions by the Respondents constituted violations by the Respondents of 1) the Securities Act of 1933, 2) the Securities and Exchange Act of 1934 and 3) the Mississippi Securities Act.

Respondents denied all of the claims of the Claimant and further alleged the following defenses:

1. Failure to state a claim upon which relief can be granted since there is no private right of action under NASD and NYSE rules;

2. Claimant's claims are barred by her failure to object within 10 days of her receipt of the confirmations;

3. Estoppel, waiver, ratification and latches;
4. Failure of the Claimant to mitigate her damages;
5. Contributory negligence;
6. Assumption of the risk;
7. Claimant's damages were caused by unforeseeable market conditions; and
8. Statute of limitations.

RELIEF REQUESTED

Claimant requested damages equal to the following:

Margin interest in the amount of $20,000.00, commissions in the amount of $47,119.00, lost profits, pre-judgment interest, and punitive damages in the amount of $1,000,000.00, attorney's fees and costs.

Respondents counterclaimed for their attorney's fees and costs and requested dismissal of the Claimant's claims.

AWARD

1. A. G. Edwards & Sons, Inc. and E. M. shall be jointly and severally liable for and shall pay to K. R. Three Thousand Six Hundred Sixteen Dollars and Ten Cents ($3,616.10).
2. The parties shall bear their own costs including attorneys' fees.

DATE AND PLACE

June 1 and 2, 1989; December 18 and 19, 1989; January 3, 1990 in New Orleans

NOTE: Suitability. Did not explain risks of margin accounts.

Number: 138MF   Merrill Lynch

Claimant: H. & M. E.

Respondents: Merrill Lynch, Pierce, Fenner & Smith, Inc.

CASE SUMMARY
Claimants allege that Respondent improperly recommended a swap between series of the Municipal Investment Trust Fund which resulted in a decrease in the monthly payout to Claimants.

RELIEF REQUESTED
$1,437.60

AWARD
Respondent is hereby ordered to pay to the Claimant the sum of $975.00; further, the costs, $25.00, which are payable to the New York Stock Exchange, Inc., are hereby assessed against the Respondent.

DATE AND PLACE
June 16, 1989 in New York City, New York

NOTE: Filed for arbitration for small amount.
Relief Requested was only $ 1,437.60.

Number: 144MF

Claimant: J. & M. B.

Respondent: Thomson McKinnon Securities, Inc.

CASE SUMMARY

In a claim filed with the NASD on July 26, 1988, Claimants J. & M. B. (Claimants) alleged that Claimants purchased from Respondent Thomson McKinnon Securities, Inc. (Thomson McKinnon) 95 units of National Municipal Trust Insurance Series 17 with a stated yield of 9.48% as set forth on the confirmation notice and monthly statement and as quoted to Claimant by a sales representative of Thomson McKinnon, Claimant further alleged that he read in the prospectus, which he received three weeks after his purchase, that the bond trust purchased from Thomson McKinnon was to yield 7.48% instead of 9.48%. Claimants alleged this was a breach of contract. Thomson McKinnon maintained that the confirmation, monthly statement and quotation by the sales representative were erroneous. This bond trust offering was a prospectus offering. The terms, conditions and yields as disclosed in the prospectus were, therefore, the binding and accurate elements of the transaction. Since the stated yield of 9.48% was an error, there was no contract formed for lack of a "meeting of the minds" between the parties. As such, the damages sought by Claimants are excessive.

RELIEF REQUESTED

Claimants requested the difference between the price they paid to Thomson McKinnon for the stated yield of 9.48% and 7.48% as set forth the prospectus. This amount is $19,591.83, plus interest at the rate of 2% per annum of $92,705.75 from May 12, 1986 to date of payment. Claimants also requested assessment of the arbitration costs against Thomson McKinnon. If any liability to Claimants was found by the arbitration panel, Thomson McKinnon requested that the appropriate remedy was the rescission of the alleged contract as being void ab initio and/or unconscionable, thereby allowing Thomson McKinnon to repurchase the 95 NMT Series 17 units for Claimants purchase price with Claimants to retain all interest earned to date and assessment of the arbitration fees equally against the parties.

AWARD

1. Claimants are entitled to rescind their purchase of 95 units of National Municipal Trust Insurance Series 17 (NMT-17). Accordingly, upon tender of the 95 units of (NMT-17) to Thomson McKinnon by the Claimants, Thomson McKinnon shall pay to the Claimants, jointly, the sum of Ninety-two Thousand Eight Hundred Ninetyeight Dollars and Sixty Cents ($92,898.60);
2. Thomson McKinnon is also liable for and shall pay to Claimants, interest on the principal amount Claimants invested with Thomson McKinnon at the rate of 2% annum from and inclusive of May 12, 1986 to and inclusive of May 12, 1987;
3. The Claimants' claim for damages in the amount of $19,591.83 shall be and is hereby dismissed in its entirety;
4. The Claimants' claim for interest at an annual rate of 7% payable on the sum invested with Thomson McKinnon shall be and is hereby dismissed in its entirety;
5. The parties shall each bear their respective costs and expenses including any attorney's fees incurred in this matter.

DATE AND PLACE

June 8, 1989 in Chicago, Illinois

NOTE: Cancelled trade since interest rate was misquoted.

Number: 147MF

Claimant: J. G.

Respondents: Merrill Lynch, Pierce, Fenner & Smith, Inc. and R. K.

CASE SUMMARY

J. G. ("Claimant") alleged as follows:

1. Merrill Lynch, Pierce, Fenner & Smith, Inc. and R. K. ("Respondents") misrepresented the commission arrangements regarding the American Cap Comstock Fund and Delcap Fund in the months of May and September respectively of 1987.
2. Respondents failed to properly execute Claimants order of August 31, 1987 to sell all positions in Delaware and Delcap Funds and place the proceeds in Respondents' cash management account.
3. Respondents failed to properly execute the Claimants order to purchase shares in Government Bond Funds instead purchasing shares in the Delchester Bond Fund.
4. The above acts constituted violations of federal and state securities laws. Respondents denied each and every claim of the Claimant.

RELIEF REQUESTED

Claimant requested damages of $48,932.28 plus costs and attorney's fees. Respondent requested that all of the Claimant's claims be dismissed with prejudice and an award from the Claimant for its cost and attorney's fees.

AWARD

1. Respondents Merrill Lynch and R. K. are jointly and severally liable to and shall pay to the Claimant J. G. $14,454.00;
2. The parties shall bear their own respective costs and attorney's fees.

DATE AND PLACE

August 23, 1989

NOTE: Misrepresented commissions and failed to follow instructions.

Number: 150MF

Claimant: R. H.

Kidder Peabody
Inconsistent with
Account Objectives

Respondents: Kidder Peabody & Co. and W. C.

CASE SUMMARY

Date filed: 8/19/89

First scheduled: 4/20/89

Customer v. Member Firm and Registered Representative - Claimant alleges that Respondent broker induced him to liquidate his portfolio of Putnam & Kemper Option Funds to invest in "Oil & Gas Trust" in a margin account. Claimant further alleges to be an unsophisticated investor. The advice given was unsuitable and inconsistent with the stated account objectives and prior course of dealing.

AWARD

The Claimant is to be awarded $5,000.00 and all costs are to be divided equally.

DATE AND PLACE

November 3, 1989 in Philadelphia, Pennsylvania

NOTE: Important: broker's advice was inconsistent with the stated account objectives and prior course of dealings.

CHAPTER 10

ARBITRATION AWARDS - STOCKS AND OPTIONS

Number: 301SO

Claimant: KMK

Respondents: CTW, Merrill Lynch, Pierce, Fenner and Smith

CASE SUMMARY
In a claim filed with the NASD on September 15, 1987, Claimants alleged that Respondents Merrill Lynch Pierce Fenner & Smith and CTW purchased speculative and unsuitable LTV Corp. cumulative convertible Preferred Stock for KMK's IRA accounts and Entex Energy Development for the KMK's joint account. Merrill Lynch and CTW denied the allegations of the claim and asserted various affirmative defenses including but not limited to estoppel, ratification, contributory negligence and failure to mitigate damages.

RELIEF REQUESTED
KMK requested damages of $12,500 plus a gain on that money calculated with respect to the Standard & Poor's 500 index. Merrill Lynch and CTW requested dismissal of the claim and that the costs of the proceeding be assessed against KMK.

AWARD
The arbitration panel, having considered the pleadings, the testimony, and the evidence presented at the hearing, has decided in full and final resolution of the issues submitted for determination as follows:

The Respondents Merrill Lynch and CTW are liable for and shall pay to KMK, jointly, the total sum of Eight Thousand Two Hundred Ninety-Six Dollars and Sixty- Nine Cents ($8,296.69) which sum is apportioned as follows;

a.   Merrill Lynch is liable for and shall pay to KMK, jointly the sum of Four Thousand Nine Hundred Seventy-Eight Dollars and One Cent ($4,978.01);

b.   CTW is liable for and shall pay to KMK, jointly the sum of Three Thousand Eight Hundred Eighteen Dollars and Sixty-Eight Cents ($3,318.68).

DATE AND PLACE
October 5 and 6, 1989 in St. Louis, Missouri.

NOTE: Suitability. Broker was personally liable.

Number: 302SO

Claimant: JKC

Respondents: First Affiliated Securities, Inc. and TG

SUMMARY OF ISSUES
This case was filed on December 9, 1987. Claimant JKC alleges that Respondents First Affiliated Securities, Inc. and TG made unsuitable investments in her account, such as, limited partnerships, speculative securities and options with the use of margin. Said investments were allegedly made without regard to Claimants objectives which were income generation and safety of principal. Respondents allege that Claimant had investment experience and all trades in her account were either at her direction or with her consent and knowledge.

DAMAGES AND RELIEF REQUESTED
Claimants seek general damages according to proof; interest on said sum; punitive damages; costs and attorneys' fees. Respondents seek dismissal of the claim in its entirety.

DAMAGES AND RELIEF AWARDED
1. First Affiliated Securities, Inc. and TG are jointly and severally liable and shall pay to Claimant the principal sum of Fifty-One Thousand Two Hundred Dollars and No Cents ($51,200.00) and interest there on at the rate of 8% annum from April 23, 1986, until paid in full.
2. Respondent TG is solely liable and shall pay to claimant the sum of Eight Thousand, Eight Hundred Dollars and No Cents ($8,800.00) plus interest thereon at the rate of 8% per annum from April 23, 1986 until paid in full.
3. Respondent First Affiliated Securities, Inc. is solely liable and shall pay to Claimant the sum of Twenty Thousand Dollars and No Cents ($20,000.00) plus interest thereon at the rate of 8% per annum from April 23, 1986 until paid in full.

DATE AND PLACE
October 11 and 18, 1989 in Los Angeles, California.

NOTE: Suitability. Broker was personally liable.

Number: 304SO

Claimant: FDF

Respondents: PaineWebber, Inc., RD and FOB

CASE SUMMARY
Claimant FD alleged that Respondents PaineWebber, Inc. ("PaineWebber"), RD, and FOD, were liable for: misrepresentation; churning; violations of Federal and Florida Securities Laws; breach of fiduciary duty; fraud and negligence, either directly or under the theory of Respondent superior. Additionally, Claimant alleged that PaineWebber and FOB were liable for negligent supervision. Respondents alleged that FOB was advised of all the risks; made the decision to exercise his employee stock options and invest in speculative stocks; was suitable for the trading he engaged in and authorized all transactions. Respondents asserted the affirmative defenses of waiver; estoppel; failure to mitigate damages; comparative negligence; negligence; failure to rely on the statements or omissions; lack of proximate cause; assumption of risk and statute of limitations.

RELIEF REQUESTED
Claimant requested damages in the amount of $85,061.64 plus interest, punitive damages, attorney's fees and other costs. Respondents requested dismissal of the claim.

AWARD
Respondents PaineWebber, RD, and FOB are hereby liable, jointly and severally, and shall pay to the Claimant the amount of Sixty Three Thousand Seven Hundred Ninety Six and 23/100 ($63,796.23) Dollars inclusive of interest at the legal rate of 12% per annum.

DATE AND PLACE
September 9th and 19th in Ft. Lauderdale, Florida.

NOTE: Misrepresentation, churning, and negligence.

95

Number: 305SO

Claimant: HR

Respondents: Dean Witter Reynolds, Inc. and AO

CASE SUMMARY

This claim was filed on August 29, 1988 and amended February 23, 1989 and October 23, 1989. The claim originally named SEJ as a respondent but his bankruptcy filing resulted in an automatic stay of the proceeding as to him. The Claimant alleged that Dean Witter Reynolds, Inc. acting by and through its account executive SEJ, engaged in unauthorized and excessive trading in his account. The Claimant further alleged that Respondents induced him to enter into margin activity and trading in uncovered put and call options, which were unsuitable for him, without adequately explaining the risks involved therein. The Claimant stated that SEJ solicited the Claimant to purchase interests in 2 limited partnerships through false and misleading statements as to the quality and nature of said investments. The Claimant also stated that Dean Witter Reynolds, Inc. and AO failed to properly supervise the activities of SEJ. Respondents Dean Witter Reynolds, Inc. and AO alleged that JH was a knowledgeable, experienced, and sophisticated person and investor. They further alleged the claimant was in control of all trading done in his account and that Respondents made full and fair disclosures of the potential risks of making certain investments. Respondents stated that the investments made were consistent with the Claimant's objectives and that no misrepresentations or misstatements were made to the Claimant.

RELIEF REQUESTED

The Claimant asked for the recovery of $545,246.00 plus treble damages, punitive damages, prejudgment and post judgment interest, attorney fees, expert witness fees and costs. The Respondents asked that the claims be denied and that they recover their costs.

AWARD

Respondents Dean Witter Reynolds, Inc. and AO are hereby jointly and severally liable for and shall pay to the Claimant the sum of Two Hundred Ten Thousand Dollars, in case, inclusive of interest.

NOTE: Unauthorized trading, negligence, suitability. Dean Witter

Reynolds said JH was a knowledgeable, experienced person and investor.

Number: 306SO

Claimant: LM

Respondent: Shearson Lehman Hutton, Inc.

CASE SUMMARY

Claimant alleges that Respondent ignored his specific instructions and put 10,000 shares of Farmers' Group, Inc. into his account pursuant to put options which Claimant alleges were back-timed or backdated. As a result of Respondent's action, Claimant alleges that the 10,000 shares were put to him improperly at $60 per share and that he could have purchased the same in the open market at 55 1/8 per share. Respondent denies the allegations of wrongdoing and further alleges that Claimant sustained no damages.

RELIEF REQUESTED

Claimant requests that the panel award him $50,000, interest, commissions paid and attorney's fees. Respondent requests that the panel dismiss the claim and award it attorney's fees.

AWARD

Respondent is hereby liable to the Claimant in the amount of Three Thousand, Eight Hundred Dollars and Zero Cents ($3,800.00)

PLACE

New York, New York

CHAPTER 11

WERE YOU CAUGHT UP IN TECHNOLOGY OR THE INTERNET BOOM?

Update

These stocks and funds were hot from 1996 to 1999. Most mutual fund families jumped on the bandwagon and created these funds and generated tens of millions in management and other fees. When the bubble burst and these stocks and funds began to fall in April 2000 billions of dollars in NAV evaporated over the next two years. Some funds are down from their high as much as 80%. Many of the companies are now gone. Many of the mutual funds raised money from investors based on the fund's performance and appreciation. Some brokers and brokerage firms didn't consider if the clients were suitable for these investments.

Arbitration cases on these investments have now been filed and are now beginning the arbitration process. I've listed a few cases below to give you an idea of the types of cases that are now being filed. If clients were unsuitable for these investments, many brokerage firms will pay back part or all of the investor's losses. If you believe you are one of these investors call or email me and I will review your potential case.

Arbitration Cases

01-###34 March 2002
Claimant vs. Dreyfus Brokerage Services
Case Summary: Claimant alleged trading system flaws in purchasing stock via the Internet through Dreyfus Brokerage Services Online system.
Claimant awarded $19,196.56.
This amount represented 100% of the claim.

01-###93 January 2002
Claimants vs. Auerbach, Pollack, & Richardson
Case Summary: Unauthorized purchases of Internet Capital Group.
Claimants award: $28,908.00 & $36,691.80 in compensatory damages.
These amounts represented 100% of the requested amounts.

#01-###42 January 2002
Claimant vs. Merrill Lynch
Case Summary: Negligence, Breach of contract, and other allegations involving transactions of PurchasePro.com, Inc.
Claimant award: Merrill Lynch shall provide claimants with 2,000 shares of PurchasePro.com and is liable and shall pay the claimants $99,000.00.
Claimants requested $100,000.00 in compensatory damages.

#01-###46 October 2001
Claimant vs E*Trade Securities, Inc.
Case Summary: Claimant alleged the respondent made an unauthorized sell order causing a loss to his account.
Claimant award: $10,938.00.
Claimant received 100% of his claim plus $4,375.00 in attorney fees.

#00-###95 January 2001
Claimants vs. Neuberger Berman and others
Case Summary: Alleged causes of action from unauthorized trading, Misrepresentations, Failure to Disclose, unsuitability, and many others.
Claimant award: In excess of $103,000.00.
One of the defenses respondent tried to use was "market conditions beyond the control of respondents"

#01-###92 February 2002
Claimant vs E*Trade Securities
Case Summary: Claimant asserted Breach of contract, conversion, fraud, and other causes of action involving the stock and options of Technology Solutions Company and the stock of eLoyalty Corp.
Claimant Award: $191,000.00

#00-###77 October 2001
Claimants vs. Marion Bass Securities Corp plus nine other respondents.
Case Summary: Claimant asserts churning and securities fraud, breach of fiduciary duty, plus other causes of action.
Claimant award: In addition to actual damages, claimant received punitive damages.

CHAPTER 12

MEDIATION: TAKE CONTROL OVER THE OUTCOME OF YOUR DISPUTE

Update

When I first became an arbitrator for the NASD in February 1992 arbitration was the main avenue to resolve disputes. A few years earlier the NASD tried a pilot program with the American Arbitration Association and U.S. Arbitration and Mediation, Inc to have the parties consider mediation as an alternative to arbitration. The main reason for the NASD was simple. Most cases settle prior to the arbitrators making a final decision. Why go through the time and expense if you're open to settlement. This would be an enormous benefit to both parties. Over the past ten years mediation has become the resolution process of choice before arbitration.

Since the bear market began in April 2000 more complaints have been filed with the NASD. This means more people are open to all means to resolve their dispute. As people contact the NASD for information about filing a complaint, mediation is suggested as an alternative or beginning before arbitration. They are told that filing for arbitration doesn't negate their proceeding with mediation first; or that beginning with mediation doesn't hurt them in arbitration. In fact filing for arbitration and notifying the respondents you want to mediate before arbitrate shows your willingness to quickly resolve the dispute. As a mediator and arbitrator for the NASD, I've found all cases filed for arbitration also qualify for mediation. The most common complaints in order of controversies that are filed and suited for both mediation and arbitration are:

- Breach of Fiduciary Duty
- Negligence
- Failure to Supervise
- Misrepresentation
- Unsuitability
- Unauthorized Trading
- Omission of Facts
- Churning

Compare Mediation and Arbitration

When we talk about mediation versus arbitration it's not an either/or situation. If both parties cannot come to a voluntary compromise in mediation then arbitration would be used in resolving the dispute. The initial benefits in resolving a dispute in mediation compared to arbitration is time and money.

Here are some quick facts:

1. The time line of an agreement to mediate to resolving the dispute in mediation is usually 60-120 days compared to one year or longer for arbitration. In fact, if a mediator is available and both parties agree a mediation can be done within days of an agreement to mediate.

2. Disputes are usually resolved in mediation within one session. This is usually between four and eight hours using one mediator. It is common for an arbitration to take three days with a panel of three arbitrators.

3. Mediations don't require an attorney, witnesses, experts, or volumes of documents to persuade the brokerage firm to come to an agreement. That could be a saving of thousands of dollars. To prove your case in arbitration these expenses are usually required by both claimant and respondent. $10,000.00 to $20,000.00 in expenses for each side is not uncommon. In arbitration, I strongly recommended that a securities attorney represent a claimant.

4. An experienced mediator has an hourly rate of $150.00 - $300.00 that is split between both parties. In an average session of six hours with the mediator getting $250.00 an hour the total cost for the mediator would be $1,500.00. Each side would be responsible for $750.00. In addition the

claimant will pay a mediation-filling fee which could be $50.00 - $300.00 depending on the amount in dispute and the brokerage firm's mediation filing fees range from $150.00-$500.00. In arbitration, each side is responsible for their own costs. Attorney's fees, expert witness fees and arbitration panel fees for usually a three-day session. Preparation of documents (usually six copies of each document. One for each party, one for the NASD, and three for the arbitration panel). These are the hard costs. The intangible costs are more difficult to calculate such as interruption of personal and business life, loss of production, and the cost of emotion and stress for the preparation and duration of the arbitration.

5. A specific type of mediation that has gained in popularity is the telephonic mediation. This simply is mediation conducted by all parties by telephone. The major benefit is the savings of time and money. The claimants can be in one city with their attorney in another. The respondents, usually the broker and his manager, can be in their office and still be available to do business or answer questions for their other clients. Their attorney can be in another city. No traveling time or cost to fly everyone to one location. If the broker needs any documents he usually has them in his office. As long as each party has a fax machine if documents are needed they can be faxed to all parties.

Other differences between mediation and arbitration are the following:
• Mediation is a voluntary collaborative problem solving process. Both parties must agree to any decisions or compromises that are made. Arbitration is an adversarial process where the arbitrators make all decisions. The parties are powerless in deciding the outcome of the dispute.
• Mediator does not make any decisions. He has no power over either party. He is there as a neutral to help facilitate a negotiated settlement (help both sides come to an acceptable compromise). Arbitrators are also neutral but are empowered by the parties to favor one side over the other for the purpose of determining the outcome of the dispute (based on the facts and evidence of the case).

• Mediation is a negotiation. Mediators try to show both parties their strengths and weaknesses of their case. The mediator helps the parties define and understand the interests of the other side. Arbitrators don't care about anything except the parties' position and the evidence, which supports their respective case. The parties' interests in the matter are not as important as their ability to prove their case. Arbitrators will render a decision based on the party's respective presentation of their case.

• In mediation the exchange of documents and information is limited. Usually one party will show the other only documents that will strengthen their case in the hope to accelerate a settlement. In an arbitration extensive exchange of all documents pertaining to the case is usually required. No stone is left unturned.

• In mediation all parties can say whatever they want anytime they want. It is an informal discussion between both sides. Each side can give suggestions and ideas if they feel it will help resolve the dispute. In arbitration the parties just present the facts. Usually the attorneys do all the speaking to the arbitrators. It is formal and each party is required to testify under oath.

• As a mediator, I find the most positive part of the mediation is the ability to speak to both sides privately, without the other side being in the discussion. This is called a private session or caucus. This gives each side the ability to "let their hair down" and say exactly what is on their mind. They can vent, yell and scream and say exactly how they feel about the other side. They also tell the mediator their concerns and what they are really looking for. The mediator can also tell the party his concerns about the case based on the facts from the other side. All private sessions are private and confidential. The mediator cannot, unless he is given authorization to do so, mention any part of that private session. At the end of each private session, the mediator has a monetary offer or counter offer to give to the other side. In arbitration there is no private communications with the arbitrators.

• In mediation the outcome is based on the interests and needs of each party. If an agreement is made then it was mutually acceptable by each side. In arbitration any decision will make at least one side unhappy. I've seen arbitrations where both sides were unhappy with the decision.

The Actual Mediation

Before the mediation begins both sides should have sent me confidential information about their side of the case. Statement of claims, specific documents, plus a brief review of what they hope to accomplish at the mediation. By having the facts and reviewing each side's position, I'm able to understand and control the direction of the mediation. The mediation begins when the mediator calls everyone into the room. The room is usually a conference room with a large table and chairs. Each party sits on their respective side. The mediator is usually at the head of the table at this time. When I'm the mediator I begin by trying to put all parties at ease. Usually the claimant is nervous since this is their first time at mediation. The brokerage firms representatives are usually used to the process. I begin by introducing myself and having all the parties introduce themselves. I ask both sides for permission if they mind if I speak to them by their first name. This tactic puts them more at ease. Next I explain mediation and how the process works. I look at both sides equally as I explain it. This tactic makes both sides feel comfortable. One side isn't being treated better then the other. I thank both parties for choosing mediation and say it shows both parties willingness to try to settle this matter. I state mediation had a success settlement rate of over 80% in 2002. I explain that both sides will have an opening statement and that after the statements I will begin by speaking to each side privately. Each party at any time can say whatever they want. I am here as a neutral. Nether party has to accept any dollar amount offered by the other side. Understand that as a mediator I will do almost anything, whatever each party wants if it helps to resolve the dispute with a successful settlement.

At the end of the opening statements I ask if anyone has anything else to say at this time before we begin. Everyone usually says no. I then make one last statement that concerns both sides. I say, **"after reviewing the** information both sides gave me and if I was an arbitrator on this case and had to make a decision based on this information I promise you one side would not be happy with my decision". This is a true statement; in all the cases that I've mediated one side always had a stronger case then the other. This statement usually encourages both sides to compromise a little more since they are uncertain of how strong their case is. After that I begin the private sessions. I usually ask the respondents to go to another room and begin the private sessions with the claimant.

Negotiation from Strength in a Mediation
If both sides agree to mediate the dispute you must begin to gather as much information as you can to prove your case. Begin by collecting all your confirmations and statements. Try to remember all conversations and gather any additional documents. As I stated in my book, the type of documents that can help you in arbitration can help you negotiate from strength in mediation. Here are some examples:
• If your account form states your investment objective is income and safety of principal and the broker bought you technology or internet stocks or mutual funds it's possible the broker breached his fiduciary duty and also you might be unsuitable for the investment. Show the other side your account form.
• If your account form states you have a liquid net worth of $100,000.00 and the broker brought 40%of your net worth of a sector mutual fund, the broker might have breached his fiduciary duty and you might be unsuitable for the investment. Show the other side your account form
• Any hand written memos from the broker stating why the investment would be good for you. Show the other side the note.
• Any articles from any publications showing your investment has more risk or is more aggressive than what your account form states you should be invested in. Show the other side the articles. These are just a few examples on how you can deal from strength in mediation.

Chapter 13

Frequent Questions from
Investors

Over the past twelve years, I have been a financial author and columnist. I have written many columns and articles for newspapers and magazines on resolving investment disputes, securities arbitration, and the rights of the investor. I have received many questions from concerned investors. Below are the most frequent questions and their concerns. Where applicable, I have included actual arbitration awards that relate to the questions:

QUESTION
I get calls from many brokers wanting my business. They all promise me top service and good value. One particular broker said he worked for a major national firm and was a bond specialist, and said he was trained and totally competent to handle high net worth individuals. Can I believe that if a person works for a national firm that he's trained and competent in what he's doing?

ANSWER
When I worked for Dean Witter in 1984, the training program for brokers was three months preparing for the series seven license, followed by learning the different products the firm sold. Today the industry has become so competitive and costly they want the broker to start cold calling for prospective clients as soon as possible. Time and experience and learning from other brokers helps the broker become competent. There is no assurance that a broker working for a major brokerage firm is competent or

honest in the information he is giving.

Case in point F.B. against Brokerage Firm and broker. Arbitrators awarded claimant not only compensatory damages but also punitive damages relating to the brokers conduct with claimants account. Arbitrators believed the broker was not competent for the following reasons:

1- Broker testified that in her opinion, margin did not increase risk.

2- Broker testified repeatedly that she felt that an investment operation was profitable if it resulted in net realized gains (irrespective of the fact that there might be unrealized losses).

3- Broker testified that she let losses run (in spite of otherwise active trading) because stocks "always come back".

Arbitrators also felt broker was dishonest and devious for the following reasons:

1- Deliberately checking all investment objective boxes in order to circumvent appropriate supervision.

2- Entering a false $1million net worth on new account papers at a different firm to create the impression of success for a naïve client.

3- Falsifying the options experience of client to provide greater trading latitude.

4- Deceptive reporting of account results-annualizing a two month realized gain total and offering it as an account return.

QUESTION

I bought a zero-coupon bond from my broker. When I asked what the commission would be, he told me it wouldn't be more than one percent, which was acceptable. Two weeks later my statement arrived. The amount of money I paid for the bonds was down almost five percent. Interest rates had not moved within the two weeks so I knew it wasn't the price fluctuation of the bonds but the commission. Do I have any recourse if the broker tells me one price yet charges me more.?

ANSWER

Bonds are bought and sold " NET " with a markup-markdown. This means the commission you pay is included in the price of the bonds. There is no way you will know the actual commission being charged, unlike stock and mutual fund transactions. Your problem is your broker probably gave you the price of the commission on the face value of the bonds, not the dollar amount you actually paid. One percent on the face value could be five percent or more on the value of a deep discount bond, like your zero coupon bond. An example, a 100,000.00 bond with $1,000 in commission is one percent. But a 100,000.00 zero coupon bond which matures in twenty five years might cost $20,000.00. Now the $1,000 commission is five percent of your actual cost, which could be an excessive commission.

B.C. against Brokerage Firm
Claimant purchased $60,000.00 face amount stripped zero coupon treasury bonds, maturing in thirty years. Since the price of the bonds was only a fraction of the face value, claimant felt $600.00 commission was excessive. Arbitrators agreed. November,1989, New York.

Question

My broker is recommending I sell the mutual fund I am in and buy another one which is doing better. He told me there would be a sale charge when I buy the new fund. He wants me to sign something called a "switch letter". Can you give me advice on whether I should sign it?

ANSWER

Your broker is following the correct procedure. When switching funds of different families a switch letter states you understand there is a sales charge involved when selling one fund and buying a different fund. It should also state your investment objective is suitable for the new fund, and you are switching because your broker says you were unable to exchange within your original family of funds to meet your new objectives.

QUESTION
I am a widow age 71 and live off the assets of my husband's estate which are substantial. My broker is the same broker my husband used when he was alive and trusted him implicitly. Two years ago my broker recommended that I give him power of attorney to trade my account. This seemed to make sense since I never understood any of the securities he bought and sold so there was no reason for him to call me before each trade. Even through I don't understand the statements the broker sends me, I can see my net worth has gone down every month over the last year, and my net worth is down over $60,000.00. Was I wrong giving him power of attorney? Should I see a lawyer?

ANSWER
Your broker may not have been worthy of the trust your husband or you put in him. It is seldom necessary for an investor to give a power of attorney to a broker. You should be the ultimate decision maker of your account. If you don't understand all the facts of the transaction your broker is recommending, make an appointment to meet in person and have him explain it to you. If you still can't understand his recommendations, perhaps his strategy is too sophisticated in light of your age and investment objectives. Ask him to give you a brochure or prospectus and take it to another broker or your accountant for their opinion. You may also be able to recover damages for the type of trading he undertook. In the case T.& P.T. against Brokerage Firm and brokers, an arbitration panel awarded the claimant damages for the broker's trading of options and speculative securities pursuant to a power of attorney. December,1989, Florida.

QUESTION
I inherited municipal bonds that my husband had purchased when he passed away. When they matured , we

were not able to get as high a rate so the broker said I should go on margin so I could purchase almost three times as many bonds and therefore generate greater income. He said that because the bonds were top quality, I was completely protected. Recently, I got a margin telegram and since I didn't have the money to pay off the margin bill, the brokerage firm liquidated a lot of my bonds. Now My account is worth much less than had I just purchased new bonds at the lower rate. What happened, was I defrauded?

ANSWER
No matter how conservative the investment, once it is purchased on margin it assumes substantially more risk. Margin is when you borrow money from the brokerage firm and use your securities as collateral to buy more securities. One factor which effects the value of the bonds is interest rates. If interest rates go up, the price of your bonds will go down. With quality bonds, you could borrow on margin almost three times the value of the original bonds, which means if the value of your bonds drop $1,000, on margin , your account value could drop $3,000. If the value of the bonds go down to much, the brokerage firm may require more money or they will sell off some of your bonds to cover your margin call. In the arbitration case R.S. against Brokerage Firm, the panel returned an award to the claimant where the failure to advise of the risks of trading bonds on margin was a factor.
September,1990,Florida.

QUESTION
My husband and I intend to retire next year. Two years ago our broker sold my husband some stock his firm underwrote, and guaranteed that them would increase no less than 10% in value within a short period of time. Although we were not looking for quick growth, and questioned whether these stocks were suitable for us, he

said we couldn't lose. These issues quickly went down to half of what we paid for them. Can we bring an action against the broker and his firm even through we gave in and let him sell us the stocks?

ANSWER
If these securities were unsuitable for you because of your age, financial situation, and investment objective the broker should not have suggested them to you in the first place. In addition, if you were uncomfortable with his goal of quick growth, he should not have pressured you into the stock. In the NASD arbitration case the panel awarded damages to the claimant and found the broker and the firm liable for the sale of unsuitable equity securities underwritten by the firm. June, 1991, Florida.

QUESTION
When my husband died at age 74, his broker, with whom he had become good friends became my broker. Over the next few years, he not only assisted me with my investment but helped me straighten out my finances and pay my bills, as well as driving me to the doctor's office. Two years ago, he asked me for what I thought was a short-term loan of $50,000.00. He still has not paid back the money and says it was a gift. Can I bring an action to recover my $50,000.00?

ANSWER
Your broker seems to have taken advantage of your vulnerable situation. he should not have asked you to loan him money, not withstanding any assistance he gives you with finances or befriends you in other areas. In L.W.& T.B. against Brokerage Firm and broker, an arbitration panel found the broker liable for selling the claimant unsuitable investments (limited partnerships and option and income funds). and civil theft in connection with his influencing the claimant to issue him checks. The claimant was awarded treble damages against the broker for the civil theft charge.

QUESTION

I bought a Limited Partnership and some funds from a brokerage firm. Even though the broker gave me a prospectus for the Funds and the Partnerships he did not explain how it's almost impossible to sell the partnership or that there was a big commission in the funds and that it invested in poor quality bonds and options. Because I was given a prospectus and didn't complain right away, does that keep me from bringing an arbitration suit now?.

ANSWER

No. Receipt of a prospectus or not filing for arbitration right away does not necessarily bar an investor from getting his money back from a brokerage firm due to an unsuitable investment. In the brokerage industry there is Rule 405 "KNOW YOUR CLIENT". Just because the broker gives you information on the investment doesn't mean your suitable for it.

In the case B.& J.G. against Brokerage Firm, claimants who had received a prospectus got back their money based on unsuitable investments and the broker's failure to explain the risks involved in purchasing the investments.
Florida, 1989

Question

I know nothing about securities, so I rely on my broker's advice. I am finding however that he is constantly making trades in my account. Most of the buy and sell slips that I receive do not show a commission. Does this mean it does not cost me anything for my broker to make the trades? Since I'm retired, is this the kind of trading okay for my account?

ANSWER

It sounds like there's a possibility of excessive trading, or churning in your account. Just because you do not see your commission as a dollar amount on the confirmation does not mean the broker did not make money on the trade. Brokers should not make trades in your account until they have completely explain the transaction to you and you have given your okay. In the case between HS and GKS&Co. the brokerage firm was found liable for unauthorized trades in the clients account and the monies were returned to the claimant. August,1990, Florida.

QUESTION

Because I am a widow and live on Social Security and the income off my investments, my broker recommended a High Income Fund when my husband passed away in 1988. The fund has subsequently gone up and down, and although it has provided relatively high income, I'm not comfortable seeing the value of my money change all the time. I cannot however get out of the fund and recover my principal anymore. Is there anything I can do?

ANSWER

If your broker omitted the fact that your money could have substantial fluctuation, you may have a cause of action. In a case of where the claimant was a widow seeking " safe" low risk alternatives to CDs. The claimant alleged the broker made misrepresentations of and omitted material facts in the high income government where the claimant suffered a substantial loss of principal. The arbitration panel returned a substantial amount of money to the claimant. Florida,1991.

QUESTION

Last year I sold my house and had $100,000 to invest. I told my broker I wanted income and growth. He recommended I split the money into two mutual funds. He told me what the commissions would be and what yield I would get on my money. I agreed to buy the funds. I now found out I could have saved almost $1,000.00 on the commission if my broker would have put me in the same type of mutual funds in the same family of funds. Is the broker required to tell me about this discount?

ANSWER
The broker has a moral obligation but is not legally required to inform you of this discount, known as breakpoints. Breakpoints are determined by the amount you are investing within a family of funds. A sales charge can be reduced from 5 1/2% to literally nothing. You should have received a prospectus of these funds telling you the sales charge and breakpoints..

Here is an arbitration case where breakpoints were a factor: In H.F. vs. E.K. Group Securities, H.F alleged respondent failed to inform claimant of price break and letter of intent that he was entitled to. Arbitrators awarded H.F. $1,305. October,1989, Florida

QUESTION
My broker called me about a new mutual fund his firm was selling. He said it would be traded like a stock and would give me a monthly income. What made me interested was that he said I can buy it and not pay any commission. I know my broker has to make commissions to make a living and brokerage firms don't do anything for free, can you explain what this is ?

ANSWER
The broker wants to sell you a closed-end bond fund that is having its initial public offering. It is true you are not directly paying the broker's commission. He is paid by the company making the public offering. The problem is the net asset value of each share your purchasing will be less then the price your paying. Remember, closed-end funds have two prices; the market value, which is the price you buy or sell it for; and the net asset value (NAV) which is the actually value of each share. You should also realize you would not receive your first check for 90 days because the

fund has to go into the open market to buy the bonds and that takes time. Instead of buying this new fund you might be better off buying a closed end fund that has been out for six months or a year. This way you do not have to wait 90 days for your first payment. Also there probably won't be a large spread between the market value and the NAV.

QUESTION
I've just received my year end statement from my brokerage firm. I brought it to my accountant, which I do every year so he can do my taxes. He made me aware of losses, which I had no idea I had. My broker never told me of these losses or transactions that resulted in these losses. When I called my broker and asked him to explain these trades he told me we discussed each one. That is just not true. What recourse do I have?

ANSWER
The year end statement from your brokerage firm is an excellent summary to review the entire years transactions and values. It's a quick way to find out gains and losses without having to get out each buy and sell confirmation. If you feel there were transactions that were unauthorized by you then you would have recourse against the broker if you can prove they were unauthorized.
W.R. AND B.R. against Merrill Lynch. Claimants alleged Merrill Lynch failed to follow trading instructions, and executed unauthorized trades. Merrill Lynch denied allegation and stated claimant either authorized or ratified all trades. Arbitrators gave award to claimant. February 1990, Florida.

QUESTION
I'm angry. My broker recommended that I buy a high yield bond fund. I did not understand what the risk was. When I found out how risky it was, I sold it and lost $ 2,600.00. The broker and his firm say there is nothing they can do. I went

to a lawyer and he said there isn't enough money involved for him or probably any lawyer to take his case. What can I do. Please help.

ANSWER

You can do something. First, you do not need a lawyer to file for arbitration. Contact the National Association of Securities Dealers at 212-858-4000. They will send you the information and forms you need to file. Second, the N.A.S.D. has what is called "simplified arbitration" which are for claims for $ 25,000.00 or less. The costs to you are less than an arbitration with a panel of arbitrators. Many cases are filed for simplified arbitration.

One example: J & CF against Kidder Peabody & company. Customer alleges broker failed to follow instructions to sell mutual funds. He filed for $ 1,280.00 and was awarded $1,025.00. August, 1989. Los Angeles, Ca.

Chapter 14

Columns and Endorsements

THE WALL STREET JOURNAL.

Excerpts from The Journal Report , July 19, 2004 ....Fund Fights

If you don't like how your 401(k) is handled, here's what you can do about it
By ANDREW BLACKMAN
Staff Reporter of THE WALL STREET JOURNAL
July 19, 2004; Page R7

......"One of the most common issues with 401(k) plans is contributions not being deposited in a timely manner," Mr. Meigs says. Sometimes the issue is logistics: Many small companies simply don't have the back-office resources to manage a plan properly. Sometimes, though, "it can be awful tempting for companies to be slow in depositing funds and to use the money for their cash-flow needs," Mr. Meigs says.

So how do you protect yourself? The first step is simply to pay attention to your plan so that you can spot any irregularities. *Bruce Sankin, a consumer advocate and author of "What All Stock and Mutual Fund Investors Should Know," says most people don't even take the time every quarter to look at their 401(k) statement and check the performance of their investments.* Indeed, Ms. Watterson says many of the other 70 employees at her firm were unaware of any problems because they didn't regularly check their 401(k) accounts online.

Next, it's important to know exactly what Erisa mandates. If your company picks your 401(k) investments for you, officials have a responsibility to run the plan only in the interests of the investors, to keep expenses at a reasonable level and to follow a prudent process for choosing fund managers and evaluating fees and performance. The wording is subjective, but it generally means: Companies can't divert 401(k) money for any other purposes, and when making decisions about fees and investment options, they must do cost and performance comparisons with comparable plans.

.....You can get a copy of the annual report for your plan from your plan administrator, usually your employer. The administrator is required by law to send you a copy of the report if you submit a written request, and is subject to daily fines for noncompliance.

You can also find the 5500 forms free of charge on Web sites such as FreeErisa.com (although you create an account and provide contact information). The Department of Labor also can provide you with a copy. Call 202-693-8673, or write to U.S. Department of Labor, Employee Benefits Security Administration, Public Disclosure Room, 200 Constitution Ave. NW, Suite N-1513, Washington, D.C. 20210. The department will charge a copying fee of 15 cents per page.

.....If all else fails, you can sue. Under Erisa, providers are legally responsible for any "breach of fiduciary duty" -- another subjective measure that's difficult to prove. Just because your investments tanked, for example, it doesn't mean you have a good case. You'd have to prove that your loss was due to poor procedures in setting up or overseeing your plan -- for example, if your company or provider didn't reasonably vet the investments or do comparisons to make sure its fees were fair.

"The courts quite rightly don't look at investment decisions with 20/20 hindsight," says Mr. Meigs of 401khelpcenter.com. "They look at the process, not the outcome." *Mr. Sankin, the author, adds, "You're always going to get people who are saying, 'I wasn't suitable for this investment.' And you're always going to find an attorney who will say, 'You shouldn't have lost this money.' But in fact the firm may have done nothing wrong. The question is, were you informed and educated about the decision?"*

Pay close attention to brokerage account forms, author says.

By CHARLES LUNAN
Business Writer

Staff photo/LOU TOMAN

Financial adviser Bruce Sankin of Plantation displays book he wrote to inform investors.

Do you own or rent your home? Do you own 10 percent or more of a business? How did you come to choose this brokerage firm to open your account?

They all seem like innocuous questions, just one more piece of paperwork in the annoying routine of opening a brokerage account. Yet investors' failure to fill out brokerage account forms themselves or their tendency to fill them out inaccurately can cost them dearly should a dispute arise with their broker, said Bruce Sankin, a broker who has recently written a book entitled *What Your Stockbroker Doesn't Want You To Know.*

"It is the only written document showing customers' profiles," said Sankin, interviewed at his home in Plantation, where he has started his own financial advisory firm after seven years working for full-service brokerage firms. "All the rest of the business done is done verbally. The only thing I can guarantee you is that if there is a dispute, your account of the conversations will be different from your broker's, so it's important to fill out the account form carefully."

Brokerages generally require a so-called account form be filled out during a customer's initial visit. The form lays out an investor's income, assets, investment objectives, occupation and prior investments.

In their eagerness to open an account, however, many investors let their brokers fill out the forms, said Maria Scott, an editor with the American Association of Individual Investors.

"People ... are concerned about getting the account open," Scott said. "That's a different way of looking at it than from the other side of an arbitration."

Investors should insist on filling out the forms themselves and make sure they are accurate when they do, Sankin advised.

The forms are often used by brokers in arbitration hearings to justify the sale of highly speculative investments, Sankin said. One standard question that asks customers how they came to choose their broker can be particularly loaded.

"Seminars, personal acquaintances and referrals may sound innocent, but let me show you what they imply," the book says. "Brokerage firms may say if you have gone to one seminar you may have gone to many and that you are aware of different types of investments and are probably suited for many investments."

Sankin, who worked for Prudential-Bache Securities from 1987 through April, is selling the book for $29.95. For further information, write him at P.O. Box 15065, Plantation, Fla. 33318.

BUSINESS

Sun-Sentinel, Monday, January 4, 1993

Opting out of class-action lawsuit pays off

As I have written previously, investors may opt out of a class-action suit and proceed directly against a brokerage firm through arbitration. One investor who took that course recently won an $800,000 award.

The investor, whom we'll call R.D., charged that Prudential Securities had portrayed partnerships, including Prudential Bache Energy Income, as safe and secure, comparable to certificates of deposits or municipal bonds. But in fact, he said, they were quite risky.

The attorneys who represented R.D, Michael A. Hanzman and Michael E Criden, argued that the brokerage firm failed to disclose sufficient information to enable R.D. to understand that the investment was risky.

As an example, the law firm said Prudential did not disclose that Prudential Insurance discontinued participation in the investment because of poor rates of return. Also, the law firm said Prudential borrowed money to pay out 15 percent in returns on the investment, leading investors to think that the partnerships were generating the returns.

Instead, the investors were receiving part of their own money and/or borrowed funds.

The arbitration panel's $800,000 award, included $300,000 in punitive damages.

Information on a proposed settlement has been sent to investors who bought oil and gas limited partnerships, but it was in the form of a more than 200-page book. For the average investor it was extremely difficult to understand how much money the settlement actually gave back for each unit, so it would be almost impossible for the investor to make an intelligent decision on accepting or rejecting the pro-

Also there were extremely complicated directions to fill out if an investor wanted to opt out of the class action. The investor would have to write three separate letters to three different law firms.

Because of how difficult and complicated the information was, most people would do nothing, which means they would be part of the class action and have to accept whatever dollar amount was offered.

This case shows it would be worth the time and effort to get a securities arbitration expert's opinion on whether to be part of the class action or opt out. It's your money.

Q. I have received my year-end statement from my brokerage firm. I brought it to my accountant, which I do every year so he can do my taxes. He made me aware of losses that I had no idea I had.

My broker never told me of these losses or transactions that resulted in these losses. When I called my broker and asked him to explain these trades he told me we discussed each one. That's just not true.

What recourse do I have?

A. The year-end statement from your brokerage firm is an excellent summary to review the entire year's transactions and values. It's a quick way to find out gains and losses without having to get out each buy and sell confirmation.

If you feel there were transactions that were unauthorized by you, then you would have recourse against the broker if you can prove they were unauthorized. In one case in Florida

ants alleged the brokerage failed to follow trading instructions and executed unauthorized trades. Merrill Lynch denied allegation and stated claimant either authorized or ratified all trades.

Arbitrators gave the award to the claimant.

BRUCE SANKIN
Arbitration

Bruce N. Sankin, an investment counselor, is the author of What Your Stockbroker Doesn't Want You to Know. *Readers may write him at P.O. Box 77-0001, Coral Springs, Fla. 33077, or call 1-305-346-8585.*

A PROFESSIONAL ASSOCIATION
CERTIFIED PUBLIC ACCOUNTANTS

* ELIZABETH H. BURNS, CPA
JOSEPH F. EGAN, CPA
* THOMAS J. BYRNE, CPA/PFS, CFP

* CPA NJ & PA

☐   76 Euclid Avenue
Haddonfield, NJ 08033
Tel: (856) 795-0099
Fax: (856) 795-9575

☐   249 North Point Road
Ocean City, NJ 08226
Tel: (609) 525-0011
Fax: (609) 525-0324

August 14, 2003

Bruce N. Sankin
P.O. Box 77-1502
Coral Springs, FL 33077

Dear Mr. Sankin:

After purchasing and reading your manual on investor's rights titled "What all Stock and Mutual Fund Investors Should Know!", I want to thank you again for your expert opinion and advice concerning an investment by my wife. Your knowledge as a securities arbitrator and your 'arbitration evaluation' has shown me the strengths and weaknesses of a potential arbitration case and its potential monetary value. This invaluable information will help me decide how to proceed.

I know of many clients who have investment losses over the past three years. I believe most of them do not know their rights as an investor. Many of them feel their losses are strictly due to market conditions. Until you told me, I was totally unaware of the fact that in the first six months of 2003, investors who knew their rights and first mediated and then arbitrated, over 90% got back part to all of their losses.

As a Certified Public Accountant, my obligations to my clients are to provide them with my best professional financial advice. I believe all accountants whose clients have investment losses should make them aware that they have rights as an investor. Your manual gives them this information and the step by step process on how to resolve investment disputes and, if necessary, recover investment losses.

If I can help you make people aware of the invaluable information in your manual, please do not hesitate to call upon me.

Sincerely,

Thomas J. Byrne, CPA

TJB/gbd

----- Original Message -----
From: J.A.
To: <bsankin@bellsouth.net>
Sent: Tuesday, January 21, 2003 5:12 PM
Subject: Your Book

Dear Mr. Sankin:
        Thank you for writing the book "What Your Stockbroker
Doesn't Want You To Know." While my stockbroker did not exercise my stock options on time, the brokerage firm thumbed their
nose at me and said "too bad." It was in the amount of $5,000, not
an amount to be considered a "big fish" but big enough to me!
After I read your book, I started arbitration with NASD and thought
I would not get a fair trial as is was not a jury of my peers. NASD
and your book has helped me into an ongoing settlement agreement which I will probably accept. Had it not been for your book, I
would have probably had to eat the 5K (no attorneys I had found
thought it was worthwhile to fight unless it was 50K and over?) If
you are every in Chicago, I will take you to dinner for what you
have helped me and other "little fish" get what is due to us FREE
OF CHARGE. Keep looking out for the regular people.

Most Sincerest Regards,

J.A.

September 27, 1991

To: Bruce Sankin

From: Dr. Christopher L. Hayes
       National Center for Women and Retirement Research

Subject: Book Endorsement

    It is with great pleasure that the National Center for Women and Retirement Research endorses your recent book. This publication will be of tremendous benefit to the thousands of individuals who find themselves the victims of investment fraud and unprofessional investment practices. Of special value is how you articulate a step-by-step process to utilize the arbitration process to recoup monies lost.

    As you are aware, a major mission of the National Center is to make women aware of the importance of being informed financial consumers. Your book will be recommended reading for women who attend our financial seminars. Again, we applaud this most important work.

Hallandale, FL 33009

12/11/02

Mr. Bruce Sankin
P.O. Box 771502
Coral Gables, FL 33077

Dear Mr. Sankin,

In 1986 I had occasion to purchase several thousand dollars worth of products from a major insurance company. I told their local Michigan agent to bear in mind that I was grievously impaired and that while I needed income it was imperative to safeguard the principal. I purchased the products that he recommend

As it turned out the recommendations of the agent were totally wrong for my purposes as their value eroded significantly in a very short period of time.

I had no idea that I might have recourse against the company until such time as I happened to see an article in the local paper which reviewed your book. Shortly thereafter I purchased the book and found information which encouraged me to seek redress from the company through compulsory arbitration. I contacted a firm which pursued adjustment on my behalf.

Eventually the Insurance company in question did offer to reimburse me at a figure that I thought I could live with.

Therefore I wish to thank you for writing you book which helped me so much as well as, I should imagine, countless others

Sincerely,

LAURA A. PARK

1898 Lago Vista Boulevard
Palm Harbor, FL 34685

October 10, 1995

Mr. Bruce Sankin
1749 N.W. 88th Way
Coral Springs, FL 33071

RE: LAURA A. PARK VS.
FIRST UNION BROKERAGE SERVICES, INC.

Dear Bruce:

Thank you so much for your help in my arbitration proceeding against First Union.

I believe that your role as an expert witness was an important factor in the positive outcome of my case. All of your knowledge and experience in the brokerage industry, combined with your sincere concern about the injustice rendered to me, had a tremendous impact on the favorable verdict.

Thank you again for your help.

Sincerely yours,

Laura A. Park

Laura A. Park

First Union told to pay fired worker $772,000

By DON FINEFROCK
Herald Business Writer

A Florida woman who was fired by First Union Corp. after she complained about the company's mutual fund sales practices has been awarded $772,000 by an arbitration panel that found evidence of "improper" business activities.

The National Association of Securities Dealers awarded $272,000 in compensatory damages and $500,000 in punitive damages to Laura A. Park, a broker who worked for First Union in South Florida and the Tampa Bay area.

The panel said punitive damages were warranted because of the company's "retaliatory, discriminatory, disciplinary" action against Park.

> *Laura A. Park had accused First Union of pressuring employees to sell the bank's mutual funds.*

The panel said that action took place "in a prevailing environment of improper business practices" at First Union. The North Carolina banking company operates the second largest bank in Florida.

Park's attorney, Jonathan Alpert of Tampa, hailed this week's decision, which followed five days of hearings last month in Tampa.

"For a year and a half now, I have been saying the bank's mutual fund sales practices are improper," Alpert said late Friday.

Park had accused First Union of pressuring employees to sell the bank's mutual funds to unsophisticated customers without regard to their needs.

First Union denied the allegation.

"The decision is contrary to the law and the evidence," the company said Friday in a statement. "We continue to believe her claims are without merit and are exploring our options."

First Union and other banks have been sharply criticized by customers who claim they were sold mutual funds without being fully informed of the risks.

Unlike bank deposits, mutual funds are not federally insured and investors can lose money if the value of their investment falls.

Alpert filed a federal class action lawsuit last month against First Union on behalf of four investors who claim they were misled.

The lawyer filed a similar lawsuit last year against NationsBank.

PLEASE SEE **FIRST UNION, 4C**

Fired bank worker is awarded $772,000

FIRST UNION, *FROM 1C*

Alpert said this week's decision "raises some very important public policy issues: How should the banks sell mutual funds and other investment products, if at all. Clearly, the banks need to be more thoroughly regulated."

Park filed a claim against First Union in September 1994, three months after the company fired her, seeking in excess of $1 million in compensatory damages and $100 million in punitive damages.

Park claimed she was fired because she complained about mutual fund sales practices at First Union.

First Union said Park was fired because she procured the help of an unlicensed employee to sell mutual funds to the public.

Park was hired by First Union in March 1989 as a broker in the company's Hallandale office. Parks charged that she was treated unfairly from the start.

In August 1992, she transferred to a bank office in Dunedin.

Lo que todo inversionista debe saber sobre acciones y fondos mutuos!

Aprenda claves y consejos solidos para ahorrar dinero y como convertirse en un inversionista más inteligente.

NUEVA EDICION

Lo que todo inversionista
debe saber sobre
acciones y fondos mutuos!

Por Bruce Sankin

Pripiedad literaria 1990, 1992, 2003, 2004 por Bruce Sankin.
Revisado en 1992, 2002, 2003, 2004
Publicado por: Bruce N. Sankin y Asociados.
A.Aereo 77-1502, Coral Springs, Florrida 33077
Catalogo de la libreria del Congreso
Numero de tarjeta: 90-86108

TABLA DE CONTENIDO

Sobre el autor 143

Capitulo Uno
Como ahorrar dinero comprando y vendiendo acciones .145

Capitulo Dos
Bonos 151

Capitulo Tres
Fondos Mutuos 161

Capitulo Cuatro
Que tan importante es el formato para abrir la cuenta ...171

Capitulo Cinco
Que debe usted saber que le puede ahorrar dinero ..179

Capitulo Seis
Arbitraje 185

Capitulo Siete
Preparandose para un Arbitraje 189

Capitulo Ocho
Compra Usted Fondos Mutuos? 199

Capitulo Nueve
Fallo del Arbitraje Fondos Mutuos 203

Capitulo Diez
Fue Usted Alcanzado por la Technologia en
el Auge del Internet 209

Capitulo Once
Mediacion: Tome el Control sobre el resultado
de la Disputa 215

Capitulo Dose
Preguntas Frecuentes de Inversionistas 225

Sobre el autor

Bruce Sankin es un corredor de bolsa experimentado, trabajo con Prudential-Bache y Dean Witter. Es licenciado en ciencias, graduado en finanzas y fue miembro de la Sociedad de Leyes. El señor Mr. Sankin escribe una columna de arbitraje y ha sido entrevistado en muchas publicaciones como la revista Dinero y The Wall Street Journal. El ha aparecido en la television nacional y su opinion experta ha sido escuchada en casos de arbitramento. El tambien es arbitrador y mediador especializado en titulos.

El actualmente es consejero de inversion con base en Coral Springs, Florida. Ademas de escribir para publicaciones profesionales e investigacion para inversiones de alta calidad, El señor Sankin tambien aconseja a personas particulares, planes de pensión, y corporaciones en fondos mutuos, CD's, bonos, y inversiones en el mercado de dinero.

Si usted pierde dinero en una inversión especifica que usted siente fue injusta, busqueme y yo revisare su situación.

Para más información, o si usted tiene comentarios sobre su propia experiencia en inversión que puede ser útil para otros inversionistas, o si usted quiere hacer algun comentario sobre el libro, por favor escriba a:

Bruce Sankin
PO Box 77-1502
Coral Springs, Florida 33077
954-346-8585
bruce@investorsright.com

www.investorsright.com

CAPITULO 1

COMO AHORRAR DINERO COMPRANDO Y VENDIENDO ACCIONES

Un Agente de bolsa recibe una comisión por el servicio de comprar o vender sus acciones. Si usted desea saber cuanto cuesta la comisión antes de decidir hacer el negocio, solo llame a su corredor de bolsa y él estará en capacidad de darle la información. Se debe notar que su corredor tiene la capacidad de ofrecerle del 5% al 20% de descuento. Sin embargo la mayoría de los corredores no dan voluntariamente esa información, porque significa que ellos haran menos dinero con el negocio. Por consiguiente, si usted desea un descuento, usted tiene que preguntarle a su corredor de bolsa por este.

No es prioridad de su corredor de bolsa darle un gran descuento porque algunas casas de valores bursatil pagan menos comisión al corredor si él excede cierto porcentage de descuento. Corredores de bolsa trabajan en algo que ellos llaman la "formula". El porcentage de comisión que recibe el corredor de bolsa depende de la cantidad de negocio que el corredor genera para la casa de valores bursatil. Por ejemplo, si el agente de bolsa esta en 35% como ingresos basados en la formula, el tiene derecho al 35% de comisión que la firma corredora de bolsa le carga a usted. Sin embargo, si el agente negocia la acción con un descuento mayor al que la firma permite, ellos le pagaran a él menos del 35% de comisión.

Recuerde que su corredor de bolsa no quiere que usted sepa que: **LA CASA DE VALORES LE PERMITEN GRANDES DESCUENTOS**. Algunas veces el corredor necesitara la aprobacion del administrador de la oficina. Preguntele a su corredor que solicite a su superior por un descuento mayor. Muchos administradores pueden no querer que usted sepa que la Compañia puede ofrecer grandes descuentos porque el administrador recibe un porcentaje del ingreso total que la oficina genera, entonces a mayores descuentos significara menos dinero para él.

Si usted quiere comprar 200 acciones al precio de $20.00 por acción, el costo total sera de $4,000.00 más la comisión del corredor de bolsa. En una Compañia corredora que le ofrezca un servicio completo el porcentaje de la cuota para el corredor de bolsa puede ser tanto como el 3.1% del precio de compra de la acción o $125, en el ejemplo anterior. Esto es muy costoso. Usualmente un precio justo es considerado entre el 1% y el 2%. Hasta aqui, usted puede y debe negociar con su agente.

Una alternativa para negociar la comisión del corredor es decirle que usted quiere negociar en una base por acción. Negociando en una base por acción es cuando usted paga la comision en cada acción compartida que usted compra opuesto al porcentage del precio total de la acción **e.i.** Es possible negociar una comision desde $.10 hasta $.25 por compartir el costo con el corredor. **Digale a su agente que usted esta dispuesto a pagarle a él**. Si el agente de bolsa le dice que él no negociara el costo de la comisión como usted quiere, entonces busque un corredor que sí lo haga. Siempre habra corredores de bolsa buscando negocios.

Si usted esta dirigiendo las transacciones en su cuenta, e.i. diciendole a su agente que comprar o vender, entonces sus servicios tienen un valor limitado para usted, porque esta actuando solamente como tomador de ordenes. Hasta aqui, usted debera decidir cuanto quiere pagar por sus servicios.

Usted no debe olvidar que el corredor de bolsa es un vendedor que gana comisión: El quiere y necesita su negocio. No crea en su corredor si le dice que no es asi.

Esto es lo que el hace para vivir. El no quiere perder su negocio o que usted reciba asesoria de alguien diferente. Y, si su agente realmente no quiere negociar en su precio, no se preocupe, usted siempre encontrara alguien que si lo hara, usted solo tiene que buscar.

CAPITULO 2

BONOS

Si usted pregunta, su agente de bolsa le debe decir su comisión por la compra o venta de acciones. Igualmente si usted pregunta, él le tiene que decir su precio de venta cuando usted compra o vende un fondo mutuo. Sin embargo, cuando usted compra un bono y si este es libre de impuestos municipales, la mayoria de los bonos corporativos, o un bono del tesoro, su agente no tiene que decirle que estan ganando él y su firma en esa transaccion. Esto sucede porque los bonos son comprados y vendidos con una cargo o rebaja sobre el precio de venta que no tienen que ser divulgados. Comprando o vendiendo un bono con cargo o rebaja sobre el precio de venta es preferible que la comisión y es llamado comprado o vendido "por el precio neto".

Si usted va donde su agente para comprar un bono libre de impuestos y él dice que el precio es $10,000.00 neto, generalmente el agente le va a decir que el precio incluye la comision. Sin embargo usted todavia tiene una forma de averiguar cuanto le cuesta la transacción, averiguando cuanto le pagaría la firma si usted le quisiera vender el mismo bono a ellos, por ejemplo, la respuesta podra ser que la firma le pagaría $96,000.00 si ellos se lo estuvieran comprando a usted, entonces el costo real de la opcion del bono es $400.00 o 4%.

Si usted le pregunto a su corredor cual es el precio de compra o de venta del bono, el precio esta normalmente en su computador. EL también puede enviar un cable o enviar un correo electrónico a su departamento de bonos para conseguir esta información. El además tiene otras opciones. El puede verificar en el inventario de bonos de su computador. Las casa de calores bursatil mantienen un inventario de bonos para ofrecer y vender a sus clientes. El problema potencial es que el precio de los bonos puede cambiar diariamente. Esto significa que el precio de un bono especifico puede ser diferente en diferentes casas de valores. Cada casa de valores cambian el precio que ellas consideran que pueden conseguir por él. La diferencia entre ofrecer y preguntar (vender y comprar) dandosela al agente del departamento de bonos es generalmente de ¼ a 1% como máximo.

Esta difusión es lo que el departamento de bonos le hace al bono. Entonces el corredor de bolsa suma a su comisión usualmente entre el ½% y 4%. **Usted como cliente, probablemente ignora esto, que el corredor puede cargar o rebajar el bono dependiendo de lo que él piensa que usted lo comprara o lo vendera.** En la compra o venta del mismo bono, el corredor y la casa de valores bursatil en conjunto pueden recibir maximo el 6% en el negocio.

Su corredor de bolsa no desea que usted sepa que usted puede negociar el precio del bono. Cuando él le da el precio del bono usted usualmente pude negociar entre el ¼% y 1% del precio del bono. En un bono de $25,000.00 de compra o venta, usted puede ahorrar hasta un $250.00. Si su agente no desea darle ese descuento, entonces llame otro agente y digale lo que usted esta buscando. Con billones de dolares de venta de bonos diarios, habra un agente que pueda adquirir el bono en el precio que usted le asigno. Por otro lado, si su agente le ofrece un bono y, despues de llamar otras casas de valores bursatil, usted puede encontrar el mejor precio, cotizacion y rendimiento. **Comprelo.** Conseguir lo que usted quiere es más importante que saber lo que la firma corredora de bolsa hace.

UnitTrusts

En algunos momentos las casa de valores o compañias independientes ponen un grupo de bonos juntos y los venden como un paquete. Estos paquetes son usualmente llamados "unit trusts". Un unit trusts puede ser preferible a bonos individuales porque diversifica la cantidad de riesgo en un grupo de bonos en vez de colocar todo el dinero en un bono. Otro beneficio de los unit trust es que los intereses son pagados mensualmente comparado con un bono individual, donde el pago de los intereses es semianual. Por otro lado, el costo de comprar un unit trust es económico; puede estar en un rango del 4% al 5% y es parte integral de la estructura de la confianza. Por consiguiente, las comisiones en un unit trust generalmente no puede ser negociada. La compra de un unit trust es, sin embargo, sujeto a descuentos en la comisión en forma de "puntos criticos". Esto significa que por cierto volumen de compra la comisión disminuira.

Comunes puntos críticos en la compra de un unit trust son $50,000.00 $100,000.00 y $250,000.00. En una compra por debajo de $100.000.00 usted puede pagar 43/4% de comisión mientras por $100,000.00 usted puede pagar 31/4%, por $250,000 21/2% etc. (Se debio notar que su corredor recibe una comisión cuando usted compra un unit trust, aunque no es general cuando lo vende).

Cuando usted pregunta por un unit trust, su agente le debe dar tres cotizaciones, El le cotizara el precio que usted pagaría si usted lo quisiera comprar (precio de demanda): el precio que usted obtendra si usted lo quiere vender (precio de oferta); y el valor real (valor nominal) de los bonos en cada unit trust. El valor nominal es también la cantidad de dinero que usted recibira si usted tiene esa unidad hasta el vencimiento (fecha de vencimiento, si la unidad tiene precio de vencimiento).

Cuando su agente le da un precio y el rendimiento en un unit trust, asegurese de que le diga dos rendimientos: el rendimiento corriente y el rendimiento de madurez o de vencimiento. Es tambien importante investigar si el bono en el unit trust tiene opcion de compra. Esto significa que la compañia o municipalidad puede comprar de nuevo los bonos antes de su vencimiento. No tiene opción si el bono se vencio. El unit trust se debe regresar. Asegurese de que su corredor le diga el rendimiento de la opción. Puede ser mucho mayor que el rendimiento al momento de vencimiento o rendimiento corriente y usted no quiere ninguna sorpresa despues de que usted compra el unit trust.

Sea muy cuidadoso cuando su corredor le de la cotizacion del rendimiento corriente en el unit trust que suena mas alto que un bono individual. Si esto ocurre, preguntele por el precio de oferta, el precio de demanda y el precio nominal. Por ejemplo, si el agente le dice que usted obtendra el 7.75% retorno corriente en unit trust y un bono individual comparable es solo el 7.0% retorno corriente, entonces hay una buena opción que usted este pagando una prima por cada unit trust.

Una prima es la diferencia entre lo que usted paga (precio de demanda) y el valor real (valor nominal). Si el precio de demanda por la unidad es $1,000.00 por unidad y el precio nominal es $900.00 por unidad, usted esta pagando $100.00 por unidad o 10 % más de el valor real. Si usted compro 10 unidades a $1,000.00 cada una y pago $10,000.00 y usted retuvo las unidades hasta el vencimiento, usted solo recibira $9,000.00. Usted recibira más ingreso en sus unidades cada año, pero al final usted recuperara menos capital del que usted puso en el. Bonos preferentes y unit trust puden ser buena inversión si usted entiende que esta renunciando a capital por el ingreso extra anual. Cuando compra bonos usted le debe preguntar a su corredor de bolsa la clasificación de los bonos y del unit trust. Una clasificación le dara la calidad y el riesgo en cada bono. A mayor calidad, menor es el riesgo, y menor es el rendimiento o "recuperacion en la inversion". Inversamente, a menor calidad, mayor es el riesgo, y mayor es el rendimiento. La mayoría de los bonos son clasificados por dos compañias: Standard & Poors,

comunmente conocida como S&P, y Moody's Investors Service.
Las siguientes son las definiciones de Standard & Poor's para clasificar los bonos.

AAA- Clasificación del endeudamiento 'AAA' tiene la más alta clasificacion asignada por Standard & Poor's. La capacidad para pagar intereses y recuperar capital es extremadamente alta.

AA- Clasificación del endeudamiento 'AA' tiene muy alta capacidad para pagar interes y recuperar capital y se diferencia de la que tiene la más alta clasificación solo en un pequeño grado.

A- Clasificación del endeudamiento 'A' tiene alta capacidad para pagar intereses y recuperar capital sin embargo de alguna manera es más susceptible a efectos adversos, cambios de circunstancias y condiciones económicas que la clasificada en anteriermente.

BBB- Clasificación del endeudamiento 'BBB'se refiere a tener una adecuada capacidad para pagar intereses y recuperar capital. Considarendo que normalmente muestra adecuados parametros de protección, condiciones economicas adversas o cambio de circunstancias y sería semenjante a cobrar cuando existe una capacidad muy débil de pagar intereses y reembolsar capital y endeudamiento, esta debilidad es más alta en esta categoría.

BB, B. CCC, BB, C-
Clasificación del endeudamiento 'BB', 'B', 'CCC', 'CC' y 'C'esta considerado, en balance, como predominantemente especulativo con respecto a la capacidad de pagar intereses y recuperar capital acorde con los terminos de la obligacion. 'BB' indica el nivel más bajo de especulación y 'C' el

nivel más alto en especulación. Mientras semejante deuda puede tener alguna calidad y características protectoras, estos son más valederas para grandes incertidumbres o mayor exposición al riesgo en condiciones adversas.

Estandares de calidad en bonos de inversión:

Bajo las regulaciones actuales de los bancos comerciales emitidas por el Regulador de la moneda, bonos clasificados entre las mejores categorias ("AAA', 'AA, 'A', 'BBB', comunmente conocidos como "clasificación del endeudamiento) son generalmente considerados como elegibles para inversión bancaria. En adición, las leyes de inversión de varios estados pueden imponer cierta clasificación o otros estándares para obligaciones elegibles para inversiones en cuentas de ahorro, entidades de crédito, compañias de seguro y generalmente fiduciarias.

Existen tambien bonos no clasificados o bonos NC. Esto significa que por alguna razón S&P y/o Moody's no tienen clasificada la calidad de un bono en particular, esto no significa, que existe algun problema con el bono. Si usted esta interesado en un bono no clasificado, preguntele a su corredor de bolsa investigar la razón por la cual no esta clasificado. No existe una buena razón por la cual el bono no este clasificado, entonces lo mejor que usted puede hacer es ignorar ese bono y encontrar otro bono con una claisficación que lo satisfaga.

Mucho unit trusts son vendidos en el mercado secundario. Esto significa que un individuo vende el unit trust antes del vencimiento. A menudo, el unit trust vendido antes del vencimiento es comprado por la casa de valores y colocado entre el inventario de la firma. Esto significa que usted puede estar en capacidad de comprar en un unit trust que tenga un cupo mas alto, (preferente) o bajo cupo (descuento) del inventario de la casa de valores.

Bonos individuales y unit trusts tienen algo en comun que los compradores algunas veces ignoran. El valor nominal de estas inversiones es solo pagado al vencimiento. Si usted vende esta inversión antes del vencimiento, usted podra obtener el precio del mercado. Precio del mercado es el precio que la casa de valores esta dispuesta a pagar. Este precio puede ser más alto o más bajo que el precio que usted pago por él. Por ejemplo, Usted compro un bono de la General Electric por $10,000.00 que expira en Enero 1 de 2020. Si usded retiene el bono hasta el vencimiento, General Electric le pagará a usted $10,000.00 en Enero 1 de 2020. Si usted vende este bono antes de Enero 1, 2020. Es decisión estricta de la compañia corredora de bolsa que precio le pagaran ellos por su bono.

CAPITULO 3

FONDOS MUTUOS

Uno de los grandes grupos de productos en los ochentas, donde agentes paticulares ganan enormes comisiones, fué en fondos mutuos. Fondos mutuos son una simple forma de invertir en titulos. Digale a su corredor de bolsa lo que usted esta buscando: acciones; bonos; una inversion estratégica agresiva o conservadora o una revalorización; entonces su agente encuentra el fondo mutuo que satisface sus necesidades. Puesto que su corredor es un vendedor que trabaja por comisión, él usualmente inténtara venderle un fondo mutuo recien abierto que tiene costo de venta.. Muchos fondos cobran por adelantado los costos de ventas entre el 4% y 81/2%. Fondos de bonos tienen costo de ventas que oscilan entre 3% y 5%. Costos de ventas son generalmente reducidos mientras más usted invierta. Esto es conocido como quebrar puntos o en terminos simples, un descuento por volumen.

A principios de los ochentas las firmas corredoras de bolsa comprendieron que a la gente no le gusta pagar por adelantado el costo de venta, entonces ellos se inventaron un nuevo tipo de cargo de ventas llamado "costo de venta al final" o "costos de desempeño". Esto significa que usted puede pagar un costo de venta cuando usted venda otra vez su porción al fondo. Muchos fondos mutuos que cobran al final de la inversión tiene un costo anual adicional para el accionista conocido como el costo 12b-1. Los administradores de fondos mutuos dicen que este costo es usado para promover y anunciar el fondo a otros potenciales accionistas. Este costo puede ser tan alto como 11/4% por año. SI usted conserva el fondo mutuo que tiene el costo 12b-1 de 1.25% por 10 años y lo vende, usted estara perdiendo un adicional 121/2 % de sus activos. El costo 12b-1 de menos del ¼% al 1% al año realmente no hace una gran diferencia; sin embargo, nada más que esto, a menos que el fondo sea un presentador estelar, es injustificado en mi opinion y yo buscaria otro fondo.

Corredores de bolsa no desean que usted sepa que usted no tiene que comprar en los fondos mutuos de ellos. Si a usted le interesa lo que sucede con su dinero y esta dispuesto a dedicar las horas a investigar para fiscalizar sus finanzas, usted puede comprar un fondo mutuo sin cargos. Hay muchos fondos mutuos sin cargos con la misma o similar tipo de seguridad y objetivos de inversión que su agente compraría para usted con un costo de venta. Conocido como fondos con carga. Si usted tiene $10,000.00 para invertir, una opción puede ser llamar a su corredor de bolsa y concretar una cita. En esa cita, usted puede discutir sus necesidades financieras. Al final de la reunión, despúes de que el corredor de bolsa hizo sus calculus, él probablemente le recomendara un fondo mutuo especifico. Si su fondo mutuo tiene un cargo de venta de 5% usted solo le tiene que pagar $500.00 por sus consejos profesionales financieros. Ahora usted tiene que decidir si la reunion cara a cara valio la pena.. Una vez el dinero este en el fondo mutuo, la ejecucucion depende del administrador del portafolio.

IMPORTANTE! Es muy importante que al menos usted sepa, y entienda, como seleccionar un fondo sin carga que satisfaga su nivel de tolerancia al riesgo, objetivo de inversión e idoneidad, o usted sera inducido emocionalmente por factores erróneos al comprar en un fondo mutuo especifico. Desafortunadamente, inversionistas sencillos compran un fondo mutuo basado en el desempeño de los últimos 12 meses sin considerar otros factores. Sí estamos hablando de grandes sumas de dinero que pueden afectar su futuro financiero, a menos que usted este dispuesto a dedicar el tiempo, esfuerzo,

investigacion y monitorear su propio dinero, el servicio de un professional financiero calificado puede ser la mejor opción.

Si usted decide escoger un fondo mutuo por usted mismo, hay un número de recursos que usted puede usar. Uno de los mejores recursos es el **Morningstar Mutual Founds Value Report**. Este libro le dará la información que usted necesita para hacer un juicio justo en miles de fondos mutuos. Muchos agentes de bolsa usan esta informacion para escoger fondos mutuos para sus clietes. Revistas como **Dinero y Forbes** públican ediciones especíales que describen y clasifican los fondos mutuos. También hay circulares que hacen seguimiento a las industria de los fondos mutuos. Verifique en los buscadores de internet por "Circulares de los fondos mutuos" mensualmente las circulares le dan recom endaciones y actualizaciones de la mayoria de los fondos mutuos.

Si usted no desea ponerle el tiempo y esfuerzo para encontrar un fondo sin carga y todavia desea usar los servicios de un agente para recomendarle una buena familia de fondos, aqui hay una idea en cómo reducir los costos de la venta. Muchas excelentes familias de fondos como M.F.S., Putnam, Delaware Group, American, Aim, etc. tienen diferentes fondos en la misma familia. Todos esos fondos han intercambiado privilegios, que significa que usted puede cambiar de un fondo a otro al valor del activo neto. Lo que el agente de bolsa no desea que usted sepa es que fondos diferentes dentro de la misma familia tienen diferentes costos de venta.

Esto significa que usted puede comprar un fondo que tiene una costos de 21/2% y una semana despúes usted puede cambiarlo por el fondo que usted realmente quiere, que tiene un 53/4% carga ahorrandole a usted un 31/4% en la compra del fondo. Esto puede ahorrarle cientos de dolares que no le tiene que pagar alcorredor. Estos ahorros pueden oscilar entre 25% -60% en el cargo de venta. Existen dos tipos de fondos mutuos: fondo abierto y fondo cerado. Los fondos mutuos abiertos consisten en un portafolio de titulos que hacen negocios al valor neto del activo. O N.A.V. Valor neto del activo es el valor total del titulo en el fondo al final de cada dia de negocios dividido por el número de acciones pendientes por pagar de el fondo. Así es como consigue el costo por participación en un fondo mutuo cerrado. Entonces, igualmente si usted compra en un fondo abiero en la mañana, su corredor no puede decirle que pago por el fondo hasta el día siguiente. Fondo abiero también significa que el número de cuotas que pueden ser compradas es ilimitado. Un fondo cerrado es un fondo que tiene un limitado número de cuotas.

Un fondo abierto y un fondo cerrado son similares en que ellos dos tienen titulos en el portafolio, ellos dos cobran al inversionista por gastos, y ellos dos tienen N.A.V.'s; sin embargo, a diferencia de las cuotas en un fondo abiero, las acciones en un fondo cerrado son tratadas libremente en el merado abierto. Esto significa que las cuotas pueden ser compradas o vendidas por debajo (con descuento) o por encima (con prima) del fondo del valor neto de los activos. Puesto que el número de acciones en un fondo cerrado es limitado, el precio al que usted vende o compra las acciones en el mercado abierto dependera de la demanda de las acciones. Claramente, entonces hay un riesgo adicional en un fondo cerrado. No solo es la fluctuacion en el valor del activo neto, tambien en la demanda de las acciones, y por lo tanto, tambien existe una oportunidad. Si usted compra acciones en un fondo cerrado alguien esta vendiendo las acciones con un descuento significante por el valor neto de los activos, esto es posible en un mercado creciente que no solo incrementara el valor neto de los activos, también incrementara la demanda de las acciones. Esto disminuira el descuento y posiblemente pondra el precio de la accion a prima para el valor neto de los activos. Usted puede encontrar información especifica de fondos cerrados en el **WALL STREET JOURNAL y BARRONS**. Ellos tendran el precio de la acción, valor neto de los activosy porcentage de descuento o prima, entonces usted facilmente estara completamente informado.

Si su agente lo llama sobre un nuevo fondo cerrado qué está llegando al mercado yo recomiendo que usted no lo compre en la oferta inicial. Puesto que el precio del mercado es usualmente a la prima de los acivos netos. Esto es conveniente para los fondos con venta inicial y gastos administrativos. Como un ejemplo, muchos fondos cerrados que llegaron al mercado en 1988 tuvieron un precio de oferta de diez dolares. Pero el activo neto fue $9.30 (significa que 7% fueron costos). Yo recomiendo esperar de seis meses a un año para ver como se comporta, y cúal es el valor del activo neto y la demanda.

Un factor final que su agente de bolsa no desea que usted sepa es: una vez el corredor de bolsa compra los bonos, fondo mutuo, él usualmente se gana su comisión. Por lo tanto él no puede ganar más comisión por esta inversión, él usualmente es indiferente para hacerle un seguimiento a esta inversión. Corredores llaman el dinero que ellos invirtieron "ido", lo que significa que ellos son incapaz de generar comisión adicional por el dinero. En fondos mutuos su corredor pude hacer a "comision adicional" de las cuotas 12b-1, pero esto es usualmente un **10-25** bases de puntos por año, muy poco para darle el incentivo de seguir su desempeño en el fondo. La única forma para él de generar comisión adicional es por usted venderlo y comprar algo más.

Porque invertir en fondos mutuos?

Cuando yo le pregunto a los clientes porque ellos invierten en fondos mutuos la mayoría de ellos se ríen y dicen "Como todo el mundo, yo quiero hacer dinero". La respuesta no es tan simple como "quiero hacer dinero". Cuando yo les solicito que me expliquen porque ellos quieren que su fondo mutuo les produzca dinero la respuesta es diferente de persona a persona. Una respuesta que fue universal fue que ellos desean tener suficiente dinero cuando lleguen a viejos. Todo el mundo entiende que a menos que se sea financieramente independiente, ellos no tendrán la capacidad de retirarse. Muchas personas no entienden que invertir dinero es lo mismo que trabajar. Aquí esta lo que quiero decir. La definición de trabajo es "una ocupación en al cual usted recibe un pago de salario o comisión". Bueno, invertir dinero en fondos mutuos también recibe un pago. Dependiendo de el tipo de fondo mutuo la inversión de su dinero puede recibir pago de tres maneras: por ingresos por interés, dividendos o por valorización.

Independencia financiera significa tener inversiones que le paguen tanto como su ocupación el paga. Solo entonces usted estará seguro financieramente para el retiro. El problema es que mucha gente no tiene idea de que necesitan hacer para tener independencia financiera en veinte, treinta o cuarenta años. Me sorprendo cuando hablo con le gente y me dicen que ellos planean unas vacaciones y ellos saben exactamente cuanto dinero necesitaran. Sin embargo cuando se refieren al retiro ellos no tienen idea de como calcularlo. Yo les digo que de la misma forma como ellos calcularon el "juego de plantación " para sus vacaciones ellos necesitan un "juego de plantación" para su retiro. El plan de juego para el retiro se conoce como "Análisis Financiero". Analistas financieros calificados tienen la pericia y el programa para crear un análisis financiero por cliente. Basado en la información que usted les proporcione a ellos hoy, ellos le pueden proyectar que necesitara usted para retirarse. Recuerde que esto es solo una proyección. Una cosa que es garantizada es que las cosas cambian. Yo le sugiero que repase su análisis financiero con su analista financiero cada año. Si su situación financiera cambia asegúrese de actualizarlo. Esto es verdadero especialmente cuando la mayoría de su dinero esta en un plan de retiro que patrocina el empleador. Asegúrese de comunicarse con el administrador del plan anualmente. Él lo dirigirá al profesional financiero que sea preparado para su tipo de inversión.

Update

Puesto que mucha gente se queja de las comisiones adelantadas, la firma corredora de bolsa han creado "B y C'" acciones. Esto es donde el cliente compra el fondo al valor de los activos netos (NAV) por un costo adicional o costo conocido como "12-b1" costo que es cobrado anualmente. Esto reduce el retorno anual del fondoque usualmente es 1%. Los corredores todavia tienen que recibir su comisión cuando el fondo es vendido. La comisión en acciones "B" es usualmente 4% de la inversión. Si usted posee acciones "B" usted tiene que conservar el fondo por un periodo de tiempo antes de venderlo, entonces a usted no le cobraran un costo de rendimiento. Es usualmente seis años. Con acciones "C", el agente recibe 1% en el momento de la venta, y un 1% anualmente por el tiempo que usted conserve el fondo.

CAPITULO 4

QUE TAN IMPORTANTE ES EL FORMATO PARA ABRIR LA CUENTA?

Cuando usted va a una firma corredora de bolsa para invertir su dinero, usted va entendiendo que la información que el agente de bolsa le provee es verdadera y exacta, entonces usted puede tomar y comunicar su decisión sobre su inversion. Usualmente, la primer vez que usted escucho sobre la inversión fué en la oficina de su corredor se bolsa por telefono con su gente. Puesto que él es un profesional en inversiones usted acepta su concejo. Usted también asume que lo esta haciendo por su beneficio.

Un problema puede surgir meses o algunas veces años después cuando usted comprende que le vendieron una inversión inapropiada para usted, o una inversión en la cúal usted no entendia el riesgo que envolvía. Si esto le sucede a usted, y usted y la firma corredora no pueden encontrar una solución amigable, entonces el arbitraje puede ser su solución legal.

El arbitraje puede demorarse años después de la conversación inicial entre usted y su corredor de bolsa sobre la compra de su inversión. Yo casi que puedo garantizar que su corredor de bolsa recordara la conversación de una forma diferente que usted, desarrollando una discusion poco confiable y sin sentido. Para esto es el formato para abrir la cuenta, usualmente el único documento escrito que el agente tiene que lo califica a usted, se convierte en una herramienta importante para su defensa en el arbitraje.

Hasta aqui, el más importante y menos entendido documento que el corredor necesita que el cliente diligencie es el formato cuenta. Cada persona tiene que diligenciar el formato de cuenta para recibir un número de cliente. Esto es obligatorio antes de que la transacción entre usted y su agente pueda realizarse.

El formato de cuenta puede parecer como un cuestionario básico con preguntas simples, pero éste es el documento que demuestra si usted se ajusta a ciertos tipos de inversión, no conteste estas preguntas a la ligera o de forma inexacta. Puede pagarlo caro en el futuro. Antes de revisar el formato de la cuenta línea por línea quiero enfatizar el mejor consejo que le puedo dar. No exagere su experiencia o ingreso en el formato. Si usted gana $30,000.00 en un año, no declareingresos más altos. Cuando la pregunta es sobre su experiencia invirtiendo en acciones, bonos, mercancia, etc., solo escriba el número real de años que usted ha sido inversionista. Si usted esta tratando de impresionar al corredor, **NO LO HAGA!** Ahora yo le voy a enseñar como una compañia corredora de bolsa puede interpretar sus respuestas en el formato de la cuenta. Un formato de cuenta estandar contendra las siguientes preguntas.

1.   **Informacion general**- nombre, dirección, fecha de nacimiento, número de seguro social y número telefonico.
       Ningún problema hasta aquí.

2   **Residencia**- alquilada o propia. Esto le muestra a la casa de valores, de inmediato, si usted es dueño de casa, usted no es ignorante de los tipos de inversión. Támbien, si usted ha tenido relacion con un vendedor de propiedad raiz usted ha tenido alguna idea de liquidez y riesgo economico envuelto por poseer propiedad raiz. Hasta aqui, si la inversion ha disminuido de valor, usted no puede reclamar que ignoraba el riesgo en propiedad raiz.

3.   **Residencia legal si es diferente a la dirección para el correo.**
       Esto le muestra a los corredores de bolsa si usted

tiene más de una casa, esto lo indican sus activos.

4. **Empleo/ Cargo/ Ocupación-** Esto pude mostrar el tipo de conocimiento que usted puede tener refiriendose a invertir en ciertas industrias.

5. **Ingreso annual que declara el cliente. El cliente declara el valor exclusivo de la residencia familiar y estima el valor liquido neto – NO EXAGERE** Esto le informa a la casa de valores que porcion de sus activos esta en una inversión específica. Teniendo un portafolio diversificado de no mas del 2-5% del total de los activos en una inversión puede significar mucho más en una decisión de arbitramiento del 50% en una inversión.

6. **Tiene el cliente ingresos fijos – Si o No-** Si usted tiene, entonces lo debe decir. Marcando este espacio el agente es conciente de que usted no tiene ingresos adicionales diferente a su inversion, pension y/o seguro social, y usted probablemente sera un inversionista conservador.

7. **Es el cliente un funcionario, director o 10% inversionista en cualquier corporación –** Esto le dice a la firma corredora de bolsa que usted probablemente tiene conocimiento de negocios e inversiones y tambien que usted tiene activos adicionales.

8. **Ciudadano Americano.** (por favor especificar) – Si usted no es un ciudadano de U.S., pueden existir diferentes obligaciones dependiendo de su inversión y del país de donde usted sea originario. El agente de bolsa debe ser conciente de esto; de otra forma, la firma corredora, no usted, puede ser responsable por cualquier pérdida ocurrida.

9. **Clientes formales o cuentas con otras firmas corredoras de bolsa –** Esto le indica a la firma

corredora de bolsa el tipo de inversiones que usted puede tener o haber tenido en el pasado. Esto también le indicara si usted es conocedor y si se ajusta a ciertos tipos de inversión.

10. **Perfil de inversión** – Es muy importante! Si usted quiere seguridad en el capital y en la renta, **NO DIGA CRECIMIENTO!** Coloque solo lo que usted desee. También recuerde, no coloque más experiencia en inversion de acciones, bonos, opciones, etc. de la que usted tiene.

11. **Introducción** – Esto es donde la compañia corredora de bolsa se informa como usted va a llegar a ser una nueva cuenta. Las opciones son usualmente seminarios, visitas, llamadas telefonicas, comerciales, personal capacitado, y referidos. Seminarios, personal capacitado, y referidos pueden sonar inocentes, pero dejeme mostrarle que implica esto: si usted fué a un seminario que le insinuo que saliera de la rutina y buscara informarse de una inversión específica. Las firmas corredoras pueden decir si usted ha asistido a un seminario que lo lleva a ser consciente de los diferentes tipos de inversión que probablemente se ajustan a sus necesidades. Si usted es referido por otra persona que tiene conocimientos de inversion, entonces esa es una buena oportunidad para tener discusiones sobre inversiones, las cuales pueden implicar que usted sepa más de inversiones de lo que usted declaro en la forma en la cuenta. Estas son posibilidades de como una firma corredora de bolsa puede mirar un su formulario.

12. **Referencias** - nombre del banco. Si usted alguna vez tuvo un problema con la casa de valores ellos le pueden preguntar sobre sus conocimientos en inversión. Las referencias pueden ser una buena opción para encontrar este tipo de información.

13. **Poder del representante-** Esto significa que alguien fuera de usted tiene el derecho de manejar el dinero en su cuenta, también como decidir cual inversión se debe hacer. Sea muy cuidadoso con esto, dar esta autoridad a alguien más puede afectar su situación financiera para siempre .

14. **Descripción de la cuenta-** efectivo o margen. Cuentas de efectivo son las más comunes. En una cuenta de efectivo, usted compra o vende un titulo (acción, bono, fondo mutuo, etc.) y paga o recibe el 100% del dinero, usualmente en 5 dias habiles. Una cuenta de margen le da el derecho de prestar dinero de su cuenta (un prestamo) usando los titulos en la cuenta como garantía. Por ejemplo: Si usted compra 100 acciones de la General Electric a $60.00 por acción; el valor total que usted pagara es $6,000.00. En una cuenta de margen usted puede prestar hasta el 50% de la cantidad debida, esto significa que usted pagara $3,000.00 y la firma corredora le prestara los otros $3,000.00 por el tiempo que usted conserve las acciones de la General Electric en la cuenta. Como cualquier otro credito, usted pagara intereses a la firma corredora de bolsa hasta el momento en que usted le deba los $3,000.00. Comprando en margen esta bien. **Desde que su agente le explique, Y USTED ENTIENDA**, riesgos y beneficios. Esto es muy importante para actualizar la forma de la cuenta si su situación cambia, e.i. su esposo muere o se retira, etc. Asegurese de notificarle a su corredor por escrito y una nueva forma de cuenta sera diligenciada. En caso de que se desarrolle una disputa entre usted y su agente, otro factor que usted debe saber es que el corredor debe tener licencia del estado donde es su residencia permanente. Si usted le compra titulos de su agente y usted pierde dinero, este seguro de que tenia licencia en su estado al momento de la transacción. Si no, el negocio debe ser anulado y usted debe recuperar todo su dinero.

CAPITULO 5

USTED QUE DEBE SABER QUE LE PUEDE AHORRAR DINERO

Digale a su corredor que el envie una copia vieja de Standard and Poors (S&P) book. Este libro mensual le dara el nombre dela cuota, simbolo de cotizaciones, clasificación, dividendos, rendimiento, proporción del precio de ganancia, posición financiera, capitalización, ganancias anuales, más informacion sobre 700 fondos mutuos cada mes. La mayoria de los corredores, después de un mes o dos, desechan las copias viejas. Mucha de la infromación no cambia, entonces es una información valedera que usualemnte termina en el tarro de la basura. Si usted quiere pagar una suscripción a S&P por el año, usted pagara $105.00. Entonces llame a su agente y ahorre.

AHORRANDO: $105.00

Si usted esta en el mercado de fondos mutuos y esta dispuesto a colocar el tiempo y esfuerzo use Morningstar.com para su investigación.
Ahorros posibles: cientos de miles de dólares

Si usted decide comprar fondos mutuos a su agente, asegurese de que lo informe sobre los puntos de quiebre.
AHORRANDO: cientos de miles de dolares.

Si usted abre una cuenta de margen en la firma corredora de bolsa usted debe entender que corre un riesgo. Lo que usted realmente esta haciendo es obteniendo un prestamo usando los titulos en su cuenta como garantía. El precio del margen cobrado es usualmente ½%-21/2% sobre el prestamo del agente. **El PRECIO DE MARGEN**

USUALMENTE PUEDE SER NEGOCIADO. Normalmente usted puede negociar ahorrando del ½% - 1% en la tarifa.

AHORROS: Si su margen es $25,000.00 usted podria ahorrar $125.00-$250.00 por año.

ATENCION: Existen fondos mutuos que cobran un precio de venta en activos reinvertidos. Esto significa que sí usted reinvierte su renta comprando más acciones, el fondo le cobrara un cargo adicional sobre lo que reinvirtio. Entonces, si usted quiere reinvertir sus entradas, asegurece de que el fondo que usted decida comprar no tenga el cargo de reinversioón.

AHORROS: Porcentage de todo el ingreso reinvertido.

Si su corredor le vende un fondo mutuo y este **no tiene rendimiento**, o su estrategia de inversion cambia, y su corredor le dice que usted debe vender en este fondo y comprar en otro, **ATENCION!** Comprar en un nuevo fondo le puede implicar nuevos cargos de venta. Note, sin embargo, Cambiar a un fondo que este en la misma familia de fondos le puede salir más económico. Otro fondo de la misma familia le puede satisfacer sus necesidades de inversión, y para cambiar de un fondo a otro, en la misma familia, usualmente no tiene cargo por venta o un costo administrativo pequeño (5 a 10 dolares). **NO LO VENDA SI LO PUEDE CAMBIAR.**

AHORROS: Cientos de miles de dolares.

Asegurese de que cada pregunta en la forma de cuenta es contestada precisamente. Muchas personas no responden todas las preguntas, y esto puede ser prejudicial porque este es un documento que le puede ayudar en el futuro. Por ejemplo, si usted desea un ingreso regular y seguridad de capital, y en la recomendación de su agente, usted compra acciones que no le convienen, entonces la forma de cuenta puede ser usada para ilustrar sus metas de inversión. Su corredor debe deducir de la forma de la cuenta que usted puede ser inadecuado para ese tipo particular de inversión.

AHORROS: Mucha exasperación y posiblemente dinero.

CUIDADO! Muchos corredores después de que usted explica sus necesidades pueden recomendarle lo que es conocido como propiedad del producto. Esto puede ser un fondo mutuo u otro producto, que es vendido por el vendedor de la casa de valores, tambien es manejado por la firma corredora. Muchos productos le permiten a la firma obtener comisión por los dos lados, por venderlos, y el continuo cargo por manejarlos. Como resultado, la firma le da al corredor un incentivo por vender estos productos preferiblemente que por otros. Este incentivo debe estar en los altos pagos de comisión o regalos especiales si ellos venden cierta cantidad. Antes de que usted compre cualquier producto de propiedad, pidale a su corredor que le muestre el seguimiento del producto (record de rendimiento) de uno, tres, cinco y diez años atrás, si es posible. Usted lo debe comparar con otras inversiones en la misma categoria, y en esta forma usted puede juzgar si la recomendación de su vendedor es realemnte en su beneficio.

Clientes a menudo preguntan si el cobro de ventas cargado cuando ellos compran un fondo mutuo es deducible de impuestos como un gasto. La respuesta a eso es generalmente no, pero existe una estrategia. Lo que usted puede es comprar un fondo en una familia de fondos que le permita intercambiarse de un fondo al otro. Intercambiar es realmente una compra y venta. Si usted invierte $10,000.00 en un fondo que le carga el 6% por la venta, el valor neto de los activos (V.N.A..) es realemente solo $9,400.00. Si usted espera un mes y cambia al fondo que realmente usted quiere, usted estara intercambiando al V.N.A., que dependiendo del V.N.A. en ese momento puede darle una pequeña perdida a corto plazo. Porque el gobierno cambia frecuentemente las leyes de impuestos, usted puede llamar a su contador y preguntarle si esto todavia es possible, si lo es, este debe estar en capacidad de ahorrar mucho dinero.

La mejor manera de ahorrar dinero es saber exactamente que es lo que usted necesita para conseguir libertad financiera. La manera de hacer esto es tener un análisis financiero realizado profesionalmente. Un análisis financiero es el estudio y revisón de todos sus activos y obligaciones. Esta revision es usualmente realizada por un profesional financiero, incluyendo todos sus ingresos, inversiones, casas, hipotecas, seguros, tarjetas de credito, prestamos, etc. Un buen análisis financiero le dara a "plan de juego" en como obtener sus metas financieras. Muchas compañias ofrecen análisis financiero. Un análisis financiero le constara entre quinientos hasta unos miles de dolares. Una compañia, **Primerica Financial Services**, que es una división del **Citigroup**, ofrece el mejor valor por un analisis financiero profesional. Primerica, que creo un diseño de reporte financiero por cliente, no cobra dinero monetario por el servicio. Su meta financiera es: que usted quede satisfecho con el servicio suministrado en la creacion de su análisis financiero y ellos preguntan por referidos como sus honorarios.

CAPITULO 6

ARBITRAJE

Muchos clientes que han presentado demandas contra casas de valores han obtenido fallos a favor de ellos financieramente hablando. En 2001 se radicaron más de 6900 casos de arbitramento. Casos donde los fallos a favor de los clientes fueron del 53%. En 2002 los resultados fueron inclusive mejores, fueron más de 7700 fallos por arbitraje. Casos donde el 55% de ellos fueron a favor de los clientes. Esto no incluye todos los casos que han sido resueltos antes de que el tribunal de arbitramento tome la decisión. Casi el 50% de los casos de arbitramento fueron colocados antes de que la decisión fuera tomada. Esto significa 75%, o tres de cada cuatro personas ganaron el fallo en el arbitraje y recuperaron parte del dinero o la totalidad de este.

Aquí esta la lista de términos que usted debe saber puesto que son las razones más comunes para las quejas de los clientes en los casos de arbitraje.

Multiplicidad de operaciones– Esto es donde el corredor compra y vende de manera excesiva en una cuenta específicamente para generar comisión. Es ilegal si el agente genera negocios, o comisiones, utilizando la cuenta de un cliente. La multiplicidad de operaciones puede ser generada de dos formas. El primero es conocido como el "Método Looper" o índice de movimiento. Un ejemplo de esto puede ser si usted abre la cuenta con $100.000.00 y la compra de títulos en la cuenta es de $600.000.00, entonces el índice de movimiento es de 6:1. El próximo método es conocido como "Costo Goldberg/factor que mantiene el capital". Es simplemente determinando el costo para el cliente, o comisión, de los negocios. Como un ejemplo si usted hace 10 negocios de ida y regreso en un año y cada compra y venta tiene una comisión de 3%, usted necesita ganar al menos 30% en todos los negocios solo para cubrir costos.

Tergiversación – Esto significa que el corredor intencionalmente omite factores importantes o lo engaña a usted arriesgando ciertas inversiones. Ejemplo: Un fondo mutuo del gobierno, no quiere decir que el gobierno garantiza los pagos hechos por el fondo mutuo. Entonces, si el corredor le dice que "el gobierno garantiza" él esta tergiversando el fondo mutuo.

Inconveniente- Cuando sus inversiones no se ajustan a su perfil financiero. Si su perfil financiero declara que usted desea seguridad en el capital y un ingreso conservador, entonces usted será inadecuado para inversiones de alto riesgo, como opciones de cierto tipo como especulación en acciones y bonos. Ciertas inversiones financieras serán inapropiadas para usted.

Negocio no autorizados– Cuando el corredor negocia (compra o vende) en una cuenta sin el cliente haber dado la autorización al agente de bolsa.

Negligencia – Cuando el corredor o la compañía no actúan a beneficio del cliente. Esto puede llevarse a cabo pero sin obedecer la orden del cliente u omitiendo información en una inversión. Si usted tiene alguna queja contra su casa de valores o corredor, el primer paso es contactar el jefe de la oficina lo antes posible. Usted debe hacer esto por escrito. Si usted no queda satisfecho con los resultados, usted debe comunicarse por escrito al presidente de la casa de valores.

Si usted sigue insatisfecho, entonces sus opciones son: mediación, arbitraje, o posiblemente, litigio. Lo que un mediador trata de hacer es reunir las dos partes para discutir el caso y como podría ser resuelto. El mediador no puede tomar ninguna decisión. El mediador solo puede dar sugerencias.

El significado legal de arbitraje es resolver disputas; afectando a dos partes. Es importante saber que usted no necesita un abogado para realizar un arbitraje. Sin embargo puede considerar consultar un abogado como último recurso después de realizado el arbitraje. Si usted decide consúltalo busque un abogado que tenga experiencia en arbitraje y conozca la ley de los títulos valores. Si usted siente que necesita un abogado, trate de buscar uno que acepte su caso en base al costo de contingencia, esto no garantiza que el fallo sea a su favor, y persuade que si usted no gana el caso entonces usted solo será responsable por el costo del arbitramento y no el costo de su abogado. Si usted quiere saber más sobre el costo del procedimiento de arbitraje, comuníquese con la National Association do Securities Dealers (N.A.S.D.) al:

N.A.S.D. Financial Center
One Liberty Plaza
New York, New York 10006
Tel # 212-858-4000

Esta Organización virtualmente tendrá toda la información que usted necesita, y se la enviaran.

Actualización

Antes de que usted decida tomar el camino del arbitraje considere tomar otro camino que existe en la industria de títulos valores conocida como mediación. En contraste con el arbitramento, la mediación tiene como objetivo que las dos partes resuelvan el conflicto con un compromiso aceptable departe y parte. Los mediadores son neutrales. Ellos no toman ninguna decisión o fallo. Además es un proceso informal. El costo es menos que en el arbitramento.

CAPITULO 7

PREPARÁNDOSE PARA UN ARBITRAJE

Si usted intento llegar a un acuerdo sobre las pérdidas con la casa de valores, pero no fue exitoso y siente que usted intento todas las alternativas, entonces usted se debe preparar para el arbitramento. Comience con reunir todos los documentos relacionados con su cuenta y su reclamo y colóquelos en orden cronológico. Comience por el principio, que probablemente será el formato de apertura de la cuenta incluyendo el convenio del cliente. Si usted no tiene estos documentos escriba una carta al gerente de la oficina y solicítele que se la envié en menos de 10 días. Llame por teléfono haga un seguimiento con cartas semanales hasta que los reciba. Revise cada pregunta en el formato de la cuenta, analice que tipo de cuenta tiene usted efectivo o margen; si usted tiene más de una cuenta en la casa de valores; que objetivos de inversión marco; los señalo usted o su corredor; la información de su experiencia esta completa; la completo usted o su agente; esta correcta su fecha de nacimiento; su historial como inversionista esta completo; ingreso y valor neto está correcto al momento que la cuenta fue abierta; firma usted el formato de la cuenta después de haber formulado todas las preguntas; Termino usted la información del formato en su casa o en la oficina del agente de bolsa; Recuerda usted por que abrió una cuenta en esa casa de valores particularmente; y por que escogió usted ese corredor en especial; le dio usted a su agente la discreción sobre su cuenta – esto es, el agente inicio la negociación de su cuenta; y usted le dio a él la autorización para hacerlo por escrito?

Luego, junte todos los informes mensuales y confirmaciones de negocios en cuestión. Aquí tengo un consejo para usted – no escriba nada en el original de los estados de cuenta, ni en las confirmaciones porque usted probablemente tendrá que presentarlos a la parte demandada o a la casa de valores. Ellos pueden escuchar comentarios y obtener información adicional que usted no quiere que ellos sepan. Además estos comentarios pueden afectar su credibilidad frente al tribunal de arbitramento.

El siguiente paso es verificar el total de las comisiones en las confirmaciones, si usted siente que ellas fueron muy altas tome los datos mensuales y súmelos buscando el total. Usted debe entender que algunas confirmaciones no mostraran comisión. Esto sucede cuando la casa de valores actúa como principal o creadores de mercados en un titulo especifico. Pregúntele a la casa de valores que ganancia obtienen ellos e este negocio, Si ellos no le dicen, usted lo obtendrá después cuando usted pregunte por la "comisión que corre" del agente. El informe mensual le indica cuanta comisión gana el corredor en cada negocio.

A continuación reúna toda la correspondencia que usted intercambia con él agente. Él le envió información de algún producto especifico, reportes de investigación, prospectos o recomendaciones de un titulo en especial en el que usted ha invertido? Usted le escribió cartas al agente o al gerente de la agencia quejándose sobre una inversión especifica? Ellos respondieron por escrito? Después de haber reunido toda esta información escriba de forma detallada que sucedió con su cuenta. Use documentos para verificar sus declaraciones. Comience por el principio cuando usted abrió la cuenta y escríbalo lo más detallado posible. Una cosa más, si existe un particular que le pude ayudar a verificar la información sobre la demanda, asegúrese de colocarlo a él en el informe. Ejemplo, Fue usted con su cónyuge o con un amigo a abrir la cuenta o cuando usted y su agente discutieron sobre la inversión en cuestión? Su contador hablo con su agente? Hablo usted alguna vez con el gerente de la compañía? De que conversaron?

Hasta este punto, usted pudo decidirse a no buscar un abogado. Si usted decide llamarlo, la siguiente pregunta es como lo puedo encontrar? Aquí hay algunas sugerencias: Primero, referidos por amigos, conocidos, contadores u otros profesionales. Ellos deben conocer un abogado especializado en títulos valores y en ley de arbitramento.

Segundo, pregunte a la asociación del tribunal por la lista de abogados especializados en este tipo de ley. Escoja uno o dos y llámelos para una consulta. Hasta esta fase, vale la pena pagarles por le tiempo para encontrar uno con el que usted se sienta confortable. Si después de discutir su caso, el abogado no lo acepta como cliente, pregúntele por que. Si él siente que usted no tiene un buen caso usted debe reconsiderar la demanda. Si él lo acepta como cliente, averigüé cuanto cobra él por sus servicios. Si sus honorarios son por hora, indague cuanto pueden ser en total. Esta cantidad puede variar enormemente, dependiendo si el caso se resuelve en la etapa inicial del proceso o si usted tiene que pasar por todo el proceso de arbitramento. Sus honorarios pueden condicionados. Esto significa que él recibirá un porcentaje del dinero que usted recibe, sí él gana el fallo. Muchos abogados preguntan por un anticipo, Esto usualmente es unos miles de dólares. Asegúrese de preguntar que gastos están o no cubiertos en el anticipo.

Si usted decide no buscar un abogado, su próximo paso es obtener y diligenciar los formatos para el arbitramento. Usted también debe recibir las Reglas o Código del de arbitramento como procedimiento. Este folleto le dirá el costo de realizarlo, además incluirá otra información pertinente. La primer forma que usted debe llenar es el Informe de la Demanda – su nombre, el nombre de la firma corredora de bolsa, la cantidad de dinero en disputa y el pago requerido, tema a ser determinado por los árbitros –en otras palabras, su parte de la historia. Sea especifico coloque en el tanto detalle como pueda en orden cronológico y copias de los documentos para ratificar su demanda contra la firma corredora de bolsa y el corredor. Demuestre con las mayores bases posibles por que ellos deben ser responsables o no de sus perdidas. Además coloque el valor de la indemnización que usted solicita, como el gasto del abogado o castigo por los daños. Recuerde, usted tiene que probar a los árbitros que usted esta diciendo lo correcto y que la casa de valores esta errónea. Además no magnifique la cantidad de indemnización que usted solicita. El costo del proceso es basado en los daños demandados y su credibilidad puede verse afectada si usted exagera los daños. Usted también deberá diligenciar la hoja de presentación para el informe de su demanda que solo puede ser usado por el tribunal.

ARBITROS

Si usted tiene un tribunal de tres árbitros, uno será afiliado al mercado de títulos valores. Los otros dos serán personas del público que no están vinculadas con el mercado de valores. Usted tiene derecho de conocer sus nombres y la historia de empleos de los árbitros, además usted puede requerir copia de todos los fallos ejecutados en anteriores arbitramentos por estos mismos árbitros. Esto le puede mostrar la preferencia o el conflicto de intereses de un arbitro en especial. Si usted desaprueba un arbitro en especial por una causa valedera, ellos lo pueden reemplazar.

Una vez usted diligencie el Informe de la Cuenta y la casa de valores conteste la demanda, usted puede desear documentos adicionales de la casa de valores. Asegúrese de solicitarlos por escrito. Solicite los siguientes documentos (inclusive sí usted los tiene):
Forma de apertura de la cuenta.
Convenios del cliente.
Convenios de la opción.
Convenios del margen.
Todos los documentos que usted ha firmado.
Estos documentos usualmente le mostraran los convenios que se ajustan a usted y sus conocimientos en una inversión especifica.
El informe mensual de la cuenta y confirmaciones.
Estos documentos le mostraran la actividad del negocio en la cuenta. Esto puede ser impor-

tante si la demanda es por conveniencia, multi-plicación de operaciones o negocios inautoriza-dos.

Los manuales de seguimiento de la firma de corre-dores de bolsa y/o los del ejecutivo de cuentas. Esto puede ser útil si el corredor no sigue estándares especí-ficos requeridos por la firma corredora de bolsa. También puede mostrar que la firma no superviso adecuadamente el ejecutivo de la cuenta.

Formato U-4 y U-5. el formato U-4 es diligenciado por el agente cuando él es contratado por la firma. Este formato le mostrara la historia disciplinaria o las demandas presen-tadas contra el ejecutivo de la cuenta. El formato U-5 es diligenciado indica las razones del él porque y cuando el agente dejo la firma. Fue voluntariamente o involuntaria-mente? También trate de conseguir el formato U-5 de las compañías anteriores donde trabajo el agente.

Reportes de información. Esta es información que la firma corredora de bolsa reúne después de investigar los factores de una compañía especifica o los productos que ellos recomiendan. Estos factores pueden probar estabili-dad, falsedad en los informes, o tergiversaciones secas por el agente para que usted invierta en esta titulo.

Proyectos y literatura de ventas. Esto puede mostrar la idoneidad de una inversión recomendada por el agente, también una posible omisión de factores o falsedades.

El ejecutivo de cuenta paginas del tenedor y Memorando de orden. Las paginas del tenedor muestra el informe de la cuenta por el agente. Este puede ser usado para demostrar las múltiples operaciones, negocios inau-torizados u omisión de supervisión. Memorando de orden muestra en momento exacto que la orden fue ejecutada. Usted puede probar que el agente lo llamo en la tarde, con-vencer y recomendar que usted compre una inversión específica cuando él realmente la había comprado por la mañana.

La comisión corre en su cuenta. Esto le puede mostrar la excesiva comisión cargada en su cuenta. Usted también debe recordar que la firma corredora de bolsa tiene el derecho de requerir documentos suyos para apoyar su caso. Las Casas de valores bursátiles desean devolver el dinero al cliente. Ellos van a hacer todo lo posible para probar que usted sabia sobre la inversión. Aquí esta la lista de documentos que típicamente solicitan las casas de valores bursátiles:

Impuesto federal y otras devoluciones de impuestos. Esto les puede ayudar a conocer su estado financiero **Aplicaciones del crédito.** Esto puede mostrar habilidad y la historia financiera.
Cualquier correspondencia que la firma corredora de bolsa le envía a usted. Estos documentos pueden mostrar su conocimiento de ciertas inversiones y actividades.
Aplicaciones y actividades de otras firmas corredoras de bolsa. Esto le indicara el tipo de información y actividad comercial que usted esta realizando en otra compañía.
Su hoja de vida. Esto indicara su educación, la experiencia en negocios, y membresía de organizaciones o clubes. Esto puede indicar el grado de dificultad y conocimiento en ciertas inversiones.

(VI)**Lista de suscripciones a publicaciones, folletos y clubes.** Esto le puede mostrar conocimiento sobre ciertas inversiones. Otro factor que usted debe saber es que existen recursos públicos donde usted puede obtener información del personal, gerente de la oficina y del corredor de las casas de valores. El principal recurso es la **Central Registration Depository (CRD).** Usted puede obtener cualquier información disciplinaria, demandas o liquidaciones por la firma corredora o sus agentes, además datos de biografía y licencias. El número telefónico es (301)590-6500. Si a usted le interesa escribirles, su dirección es NASD/CRD, 9513 Key West Avenue, Rockville, Maryland 20850

Después de que usted este preparado el próximo paso es la audiencia. El presidente formalmente abrirá la audiencia y administra el juramento a las dos partes y a los testigos.

Usted tendrá su declaración inicial. Esto será lo que usted intenta probar. Esta presentación debe ser concisa y bien planeada, el demandado hará lo mismo. Entonces usted presentara su caso. La parte opositora tiene el derecho de objetar sus documentos y evidencia.

A este punto los árbitros preguntaran por que ellos están rechazando su evidencia. Después de la explicación el tribunal puede aceptar o rechazar la objeción. Si usted tiene un testigo que le ayude en su caso, los acusados tienen el derecho de contra interrogarlos. Los acusados trataran de reducir el daño que este testimonio puede causar a su credibilidad. Cuando usted termine su presentación o sus alegatos, documentos y testimonios. El acusado presentara su propio caso. Recuerde, usted también tiene el derecho de objetar sus evidencias o testimonios. Usted también tiene el derecho de contra interrogar sus testigos. Cuando el demandado termine el caso el tribunal tiene el derecho de hacer preguntas adicionales a cualquiera de las partes o a cualquiera de los testigos, si no hay más preguntas o testigos, entonces se les permite a las dos partes concretar sus argumentos. El cierre del argumento debe resumir lo que su evidencia y testigos han probado y que la evidencia y testigos del demandado fallaron como prueba en contra suya. Los árbitros trataran de emitir el veredicto del fallo en menos de treinta (30) días. Usted puede o no ganar y los árbitros no tienen que darle razón por la decisión que ellos tomen

Actualización

Cuando sé este preparando para un arbitraje vaya a www.nasdadr.com. Usted podrá obtener todos los formatos. Usted también puede obtener diferentes casos de arbitraje que le pueden servir como casos para revisar. Usted también puede obtener el formato de corredores U-4. Esto le informara información pasada y presente del corredor de bolsa.

CAPITULO 8

COMPRA USTED FONDOS MUTUOS?

Entre 1984 y 2000 las casas de corredores de bolsa como industria recibieron grandes cantidades de ingresos por vender fondos mutuos específicos. Billones de dólares de esos fondos fueron vendidos al publico. Muchos de estos fondos han perdido valor, muchas personas se enojaron, y algunos de ellos inclusive llevaron a la casa de valores al arbitramento para recuperar su dinero. Muchos pensaron que la volatilidad del fondo común fue declarada erróneamente a ellos o que el corredor debió haber comprendido que ellos no se ajustaban a este tipo de inversión.

Las próximas páginas le informan la decisión de casos de arbitramento cuando los fondos mutuos fueron la causa o una de las causas del arbitramento. Estas decisiones son presentadas con un resumen del caso, la asistencia requerida y la concesión del fallo. He utilizado iniciales reemplazando los nombres reales de los reclamantes, con el objetivo de proteger su privacidad. Desde Mayo de 1.989 las decisiones y fallos no son de prioridad pública, existen un pequeño numero de casos disponibles donde los árbitros fallaron a favor del público. Recuerde al menos el 50% de todos los casos entre clientes y firmas corredoras de bolsa fueron resueltas antes de que el tribunal de arbitramento tomara su decisión final. También se debe entender que solo porque un tribunal de arbitramento este desacuerdo con el cliente en una acción especifica en un producto especifico, **ESTO NO ES GARANTIA O PRECEDENTE PARA NINGUN OTRO ARBITRAJE.**

Los árbitros basan su decisión en los factores y meritos de cada caso, no en otros casos de arbitraje. El final del caso yo he anotado la razón por la cual el cliente presento el arbitraje y otros factores importantes sobre el fallo.

CAPITULO 9

FALLO DEL ARBITRAJE
FONDOS MUTUOS

Demandante: B.W.F.

Demandado: Prudential Securities

RESUMEN DEL CASO

Esta demanda fue presentada en Diciembre 2000.

El demandante afirma las siguientes causas de la demanda: incumplimiento del contrato, negligencia y omisión del corredor, y la firma incumplió con sus funciones fiduciarias.

El demandado niega la declaración hecha en el Informe de la Demanda. El demandado declara que todo el tiempo la demandante tenia o debía tener completo conocimiento de todos los factores materiales concernientes a la inversión que él hizo, incluyendo la naturaleza de la inversión y el riesgo asociado.

El demandante mando y autorizo la ejecución de todas las transacciones en su cuenta. Los demandados no son responsables por perdidas porque todo esta dentro del riesgo.

El demandante escogió tomarlo.

INDEMNIZACIÓN REQUERIDA

El demandante solicito indemnización por los daños de $17.980.12 más los daños punitivos, interés a una tasa de 12%, honorarios del abogado, y honorarios del tribunal.

Fallo

Prudential es exclusivamente responsable y deberá pagar la suma de $10,077.20 como indemnización, además un intereses del 12% por anualidad desde Diciembre 21 del 2000 como total $1,612.32 por un fallo total de $11,689.52.

LUGAR Y FECHA.

Abril 11, 2001 Boston, Massachusetts.

Nota: A pesar de que el cliente debía conocer el riesgo y autorizo la transacción, el tribunal de arbitramento encontró a Prudential responsable.

Numero: 1012

Demandante: HD

Demandado: Prudential Securities

RESUMEN DEL CASO

Esta demanda fue presentada en Julio 31 de 2001. El Demandante alega inversión inapropiada en mercado de acciones agresivo, todo lo relacionado con Internet y telecomunicaciones, declaraciones erróneas, violación de los Estatutos del Estado de la Florida, incumplimiento del contrato, negligencia e incumplimiento de supervisión.

INDEMNIZACIÓN REQUERIDA

El demandante solicita $280,000.00.

FALLO

El demandado deberá pagar la suma de $257,251.45, $256,501.45 como indemnización y $750.00 como costo de la devolución de los depósitos del cliente. El cliente permanece con la demanda bajo el Estatuto de la Florida 517.301 y es en consecuencia habilitado para recuperar los honorarios del abogado

LUGAR Y FECHA.

Abril 18, 2002 Fort Lauderdale, Florida.

Nota: El cliente no se ajustaba a las inversiones por Internet o telecomunicaciones. Además el demandante recupera los honorarios del abogado.

Numero: 1103

Demandante: EJC & HBC

Demandado: Merrill Lynch

RESUMEN DEL CASO

Esta demanda fue presentada en Febrero 5,2002.
El demandante alega que el demandado compro acciones que eran inapropiadas por su edad y objetivos de inversión. El demandante sostiene que fue debido a la opción que tomo el demandado. La cuenta sufrió perdidas.

INDEMNIZACIÓN REQUERIDA

El demandante solicita $25,000.00.

FALLO

El demandado deberá pagar al demandante la suma de $25,000.

LUGAR Y FECHA.

Agosto 12, 2002, Newport Beach, California

Nota: Lo que es importante sobre este caso es que al principio el demandante se presenta por si mismo, esto significa que lo hicieron ellos mismos sin un abogado. Además ellos recuperaron el 100% de lo que ellos solicitaron. Esta inversión fue inapropiada por la edad y el objetivo de inversión

Numero: 1130

Demandante: JB

Demandado: Salomón Smith Barney.

RESUMEN DEL CASO
Esta demanda fue presentada en Noviembre 5, 2001. El demandante alega que el agente registrado hizo negocios inautorizados en la cuenta incurriendo en grandes cargos por la venta de fondos mutuos.

INDEMNIZACIÓN REQUERIDA
El Demandante solicita $6,248.00

FALLO
Salomón Smith Barney tiene que pagar a JB $1,454.00 como fallo a favor del demandante. Los costos del tribunal son cargados al demandado.

LUGAR Y FECHA.
Abril 19 2002 Philadelphia, PA

CAPITULO 10

FUE USTED ALCANZADO POR LA TECNOLOGÍA POR LA TECNOLOGÍA EN EL AUGE DEL INTERNET

ACTUALIZACION

Las acciones y los bonos fueron muy populares de 1986 a 1999. Muchas familias de fondos mutuos brincaron al partido y perdieron que estos fondos generaron decenas de millones en administración y otros gastos. Cuando la burbuja reventó y estas acciones y bonos comenzaron a caer en Abril del 2000, billones de dólares en el valor del activo neto se evaporaron en los dos años siguientes. Algunos fondos bajaron hasta en un 80% desde el punto más alto. Muchas de esas compañías ya no existen. Muchos de los fondos mutuos ganaron dinero por los inversionistas que se basaron en el rendimiento y la plusvalía del bono. Algunos corredores y casas de valores no consideraron si el cliente se ajustaba a ese tipo de inversiones.

Los casos de arbitraje en estas inversiones que habían sido presentados ahora esta comenzando el proceso de arbitraje. Aquí les presento algunos casos para darle una idea el del tipo de casos que están siendo procesados. Si los clientes no se ajustaban a estas inversiones, muchas firmas corredoras de bolsa devolverán parte del dinero que los inversionistas perdieron. Si usted cree ser uno de esos inversionistas llame o envíeme un correo electrónico y yo revisare su caso.

Casos de arbitramento

#01-###34 Marzo 2002
Demandante contra Dreyfus Brokerage Services
Resumen del caso: Demandante alega fallas en el sistema del negocio en la compra de acciones Internet a través de Dreyfus Brokerage Services Online System.
Fallo a favor del demandante: $19,196.56
Esta cantidad representa el 100% de la demanda.

#01-###93 Enero 2002
Demandante contra Auerback, Pollack, & Richardson.
Resumen del caso: Compras no autorizadas de Internet Capital Group.
Fallo a favor del demandante: $28,908.00 & $36,691.80 por indemnización.
Esta cantidad representa el 100% de la cantidad solicitada.

#01-###42 Enero 2002
Demandante contra Merrill Lynch
Resumen del caso: Negligencia, incumplimiento del contrato y otros hechos envolviendo transacciones de PurchasePro.com,Inc.
Fallo a favor del demandante: Merrill Lynch deberá proveer 2,000 acciones de PurchasePro.com y es culpable, debe pagarle al demandante $99,000.00.
Fallo a favor del demandante $100,000.00 en indemnización compensatoria.

#01-###46 Octubre 2001
Demandante contra E*Trade Securities, Inc.
Resumen del caso: El demandante alega que el demandado hizo una orden de venta inautorizada causando perdida a la cuenta.
Fallo a favor del cliente: $10,939.00
El demandante recibe 100% de su demanda más $4,375.00 por gastos de abogado.

#00-###95 Enero 2001
Demandante contra Neuberger Berman and others.
Resumen del caso: Las causas alegadas son negocios no autorizados, declaración falsa, omisión en la explicación, inapropiada y muchos otros.
Fallo a favor del demandante: un máximo de $103,000.00.
Una de las defensas que él demandado trato de usar fue: "condiciones del mercado más allá del control del demandado"

#01-###92 Febrero 2002
Demandante contra E*Trade Securities
Resumen del caso: El demandante afirma Incumplimiento del contrato, apropiación ilícita, fraude, y otros causas de acción envolviendo las acciones y opciones de Tecnology Solutions Company y las acciones de eLoyalty Corp.
Fallo a favor del cliente: $191,000.00

#0###77 Octubre 2001
Demandante contra Marion Bass Securities Corp, además otros nueve demandados.
Resumen del caso: El demandante afirma excesivas transacciones por parte del demandado para ganar comisiones y fraude en títulos, incumplimiento de las funciones fiduciarias, entre otras causas de acción.
Fallo a favor del demandante: **además de los daños actuales, el demandante recibe por daños punitivos.**

CAPITULO 11

MEDIACIÓN: TOME EL CONTROL SOBRE EL RESULTADO DE LA DISPUTA

Actualización

Cuando yo comencé como arbitro para NASD en Febrero de 1992 el arbitramento era el principal camino para resolver disputas. Pocos años antes la NASD trato de guiar una programación la American Arbitration Association y U.S. Arbitration and Mediation. Inc. Para que las partes consideraran la mediación como una alternativa al arbitramento. La razón principal para la NASD fue simple. La mayoría de los casos llegaban a un convenio antes de que los árbitros tomaran la decisión final. Por que ir a través del tiempo y la experiencia si usted es abierto a un convenio. Esto puede resultar muy beneficioso para las dos partes. En los últimos 10 años la mediación ha llegado a ser el proceso de resolución que se selecciona antes del arbitraje.

Desde que el mercado bajista comenzó en Abril 2000 más quejas han sido presentadas con el NASD. Esto significa que más personas están abiertas a resolver sus disputas por todos los medios.. Cuando la gente contacta NASD para información sobre como presentar una queja, la mediación es sugerida como la alternativa para comenzar antes del arbitraje.

A ellos se les dijo que presentar un arbitramento no anula el procedimiento de mediación presentado; o comenzar con mediación no les perjudica el de arbitraje. En efecto, llenando una aplicación de arbitraje y notificar a los demandados que usted quiere mediar antes que el arbitraje demuestra en usted buena voluntad para resolver rápidamente la disputa. Como mediador y arbitro de la NASD, yo he encontrado que todos los casos presentados por arbitraje también calificarían para mediación. Las quejas más comunes en orden de controversia que han sido presentadas y llevadas a juicio en mediación y arbitraje son:

Incumplimiento de las funciones fiduciarias.

Negligencia
Falta de supervisión
Falsificación
Incompetencia
Negocios inautorizados
Omisión de factores
Transacciones excesivas

Compare mediación y arbitraje
Cuando nosotros hablamos de mediación contra arbitraje no es una situación de presentar cualquiera de las dos o las dos. Si las dos partes no pueden llegar a un compromiso voluntario en la mediación, entonces el arbitramento será usado para resolver la disputa. Los beneficios iniciales de resolver la disputa en la mediación se comparan con el arbitraje en tiempo y dinero.

Aquí tenemos algunos factores:
La línea de tiempo de un acuerdo para mediar y resolver la disputa en la mediación es usualmente de 60 a 120 días comparado con un año o más del arbitraje. En efecto, si un mediador es disponible y las dos partes de acuerdo en una mediación, esta mediación puede ser resuelta en días.

En la mediación las disputas son usualmente resueltas en una sesión. Esto es usualmente entre cuatro y ocho horas usando un mediador, Es común para el arbitraje tomar tres días en un tribunal de tres árbitros.

La mediación no requiere un abogado, testigos, expertos, o volúmenes de documentos para persuadir a la firma corredora de bolsa para llegar a un acuerdo. Esto puede ser ahorrando miles de dólares. Los gastos en el arbitraje usualmente se comparten entre los dos; demandante y demandado. De $10,000.00 a $20,000.00 en gastos por cada parte no es fuera de lo común. En el arbitraje yo fuertemente recomiendo que un abogado de títulos valores represente la demanda.

Un mediador experimentado tiene unos honorarios por

hora de $150.00 a $300.00 esto es dividido entre las dos partes. En una reunión promedio de seis horas con el mediador recibiendo $250.00 por hora, el costo total del mediador seria de $1,500. Cada parte será responsable por $750.00. Además el demandante pagara el costo de registrar la mediación que puede ser de $50.00 a $300.00 dependiendo de la cantidad en disputa y los costos de la firma corredora de bolsa están en un rango de $150.00 a $300.00. En el arbitraje cada parte es responsable por sus propios costos. Los costos del abogado, el costo de los testigos expertos y el costo usualmente de sesiones de tres días del tribunal de arbitramento. Preparación de los documentos (usualmente seis copias de cada documento, una por cada parte, una para el NASD, y tres para el tribunal de arbitramento) Estos son los costos tangibles. Los costos intangibles son más difíciles de calcular por eventos como interrupción en los negocios y en la vida privada, perdida de producción y el costo de emoción y estrés por la preparación y duración del arbitramento.

Un tipo de mediación especifico que ha ganado popularidad es la mediación telefónica. Esto simplemente es una mediación conducida por todas las partes por teléfono. El mayor beneficio es el ahorro en tiempo y dinero. El demandante puede estar en una ciudad con su abogado en otra. Los demandados, usualmente el corredor y su gerente, pueden estar en su oficina y continuar con sus negocios y contestando preguntas a otros clientes, el abogado de la firma también puede estar en otra ciudad. No se gasta ni tiempo ni dinero todos viajando a un solo lugar. Si el corredor necesita cualquier documento, él usualmente los tiene en su oficina. Solo se necesita que cada parte tenga una maquina para enviar fax, ellos pueden enviar documentos solicitado vía fax a todas las partes.

La mediación es un proceso para resolver problemas colaborando voluntariamente. Las dos partes deben estar de acuerdo en cualquier decisión o compromiso que se haga. Arbitraje es un proceso adverso donde los árbitros toman todas las decisiones. Las partes pierden el poder de decidir el resultado de la disputa.

Los mediadores no toman ninguna decisión, ellos no tiene

poder sobre ninguna de las partes. Le es neutral ayudando a facilitar la negociación del convenio (ayudar a dos partes en un compromiso aceptable). Los árbitros también son neutrales pero las partes los facultaron para favorecer una parte sobre la otra con el propósito de determinar el resultado de la disputa. (Basado en factores y evidencia del caso).

La mediación es una negociación. Los mediadores tratan de mostrar a las partes las fortalezas y debilidades del caso. El mediador le ayuda a las partes a definir y entender el interés de la otra parte. A los árbitros no les interesa nada a excepción de la posición de las partes y la evidencia, que respalda el respectivo caso. El interés de las partes en el asunto no es tan importante como su habilidad para probar el caso. Los árbitros tomaran la decisión basada en la presentación respectiva de cada parte en el caso. En la mediación él intercambió de documentos e información es limitado. Usualmente una parte le enseñara al otro solo los documentos que fortalecerán el caso con la esperanza de acelerar un acuerdo. En un arbitraje extensivo usualmente se requiere un intenso intercambio de documentos pertenecientes al caso.

En la mediación todas las partes pueden decir lo que ellos deseen en el momento que ellos quieran. Es una discusión informal entre las dos partes. Cada parte puede dar sugerencias e ideas si ellos sienten que pueden ayudar a resolver la disputa, en el arbitraje las partes solo informan los hechos. Usualmente los abogados son los que le hablan a los árbitros. Es una manera formal y se requiere que cada parte testifique ante juramento.

Como mediador yo encontré como la parte más positiva de la mediación es la habilidad de hablar con cada parte en privado, sin la otra parte participando en la discusión. Esto es llamado sesión privada o junta de dirigentes. Esto le da a cada parte la habilidad de decir exactamente lo que esta en sus mentes. Ellos pueden desahogarse, gritar y chillar y decir exactamente como se sienten sobre la otra parte. Ellos también le dicen al mediador sus quejas y que es lo que de verdad ellos están buscando. El mediador le puede decir a la otra parte sus preocupaciones sobre el caso basado en los hechos de la otra parte. Todas las sesiones privadas son privadas y confidenciales. El mediador no puede, a menos que él reciba la autorización, mencionar cualquier parte de la sesión privada, Al final de cada sesión privada el mediador tiene una oferta monetaria u oferta propuesta para llevarla a la otra parte. En arbitraje no existen comunicaciones privadas con los árbitros. En la mediación el resultado es basado en el interés y necesidad de cada parte. Si se llega a un acuerdo debe ser mutuamente aceptado por cada parte. En el arbitraje cualquier decisión hará que al menos una parte no se sienta feliz. Yo he sido arbitro donde las dos partes quedaron inconformes con la decisión.

Una mediación real.
Antes de que la mediación comience las dos partes deben enviarme información confidencial sobre su lado del caso. Informe de la demanda, documentos específicos, además un breve resumen de que esperan ellos lograr con la mediación. Teniendo los hechos y revisando cada lado del caso, yo estoy en capacidad de entender y controlar la dirección de la mediación. La mediación comienza cuando el mediador llama a todas las personas al salón, El salón es usualmente un salón de conferencias con una mesa grande y sillas. Cada parte se sienta en su respectivo lado. El mediador es usualmente la cabeza de la mesa en ese momento. Cuando yo soy el mediador yo comienzo tratando de que las dos partes se sientan cómodas. Usualmente el demandante es nervioso porque esta es su primera vez en una mediación. Los representantes de la firma corredora de bolsa usualmente son familiares al proceso. Yo comienzo por presentarme y le solicito a las partes que también ellos lo hagan. Yo solicito a las dos partes si les puedo llamar por su nombre. Esta táctica los hace sentir más tranquilos. Como siguiente paso les explico la mediación y el procedimiento a seguir. Yo miro las dos partes por igual mientras lo explico. Esta táctica hace que las dos partes se sientan cómodas. Ninguna parte se trata mejor que la otra. Yo le agradezco a las dos partes por

escoger la mediación y lo digo demostrando a las dos partes complacencia por tratar de resolver este caso. Yo diría que la mediación tuvo una tasa de liquidación satisfactoria del 80% en el 2002.

Yo le explico a las dos partes que tendremos una declaración abierta y que después de las declaraciones yo comenzare a hablar con cada parte en privado. Cualquier parte en cualquier momento pueden decir lo que ellos deseen. Yo estoy aquí en una posición neutral. Ninguna de las partes tiene que aceptar la cantidad de dólares ofrecida por la otra parte. Entienda que como mediador yo haré casi todo, lo que cada parte desee si esto ha de ayudar a resolver la disputa con una liquidación satisfactoria.

Al final de las declaraciones abiertas Yo pregunto si alguien tiene algo más que decir en este momento antes de comenzar. Usualmente todo el mundo dice que no. Entonces yo hago una aclaración final que interesa a las dos partes. Yo digo, **"después de revisar la información que las dos partes me dieron y si yo soy un arbitro en este caso y tengo que tomar la decisión basado en esta información yo les prometo que una parte no quedara contenta con la decisión"**. Esto es verdadero; en todos los casos que yo he sido mediador una parte siempre tiene un caso mejor soportado que la otra. Esta información usualmente estimula las dos partes a comprometerse un poquito más por que ellos tienen incierto que tan fuerte es su caso. Después de eso yo comienzo las sesiones privadas con el demandante.

Como negociar con fuerza en una mediación.
Si las dos partes están de acuerdo en negociar la disputa usted debe comenzar a reunir toda la información con la que usted pueda probar su caso. Comience por reunir todas sus confirmaciones y reportes. Trate de recordar todas las conversaciones y reúna cualquier documento adicional. Como yo presento en mi libro, el tipo de documentos que le pueden ayudar en el arbitraje pueden ayudarle para negociar con fuerza en la mediación. Aquí hay algunos ejemplos.

- Si su formato de cuenta declara que sus objetivos de inversión son ingreso y seguridad de capital y el corredor le compro acciones del área tecnológica o de Internet o fondos mutuos es posible que él corredor haya incumplido su deber fiduciario y también usted puede ser inadecuado para la inversión. Muestra la otra cara de su formato de cuenta.

Si su formato de cuenta presenta un liquido neto por el valor de $100,000.00 y él corredor lo llevo a un 40% de su valor neto en un sector de fondo mutuos, el corredor pudo haber incumplido su función fiduciaria y usted puede ser inapropiado para esa inversión. Muestra el otro lado del formato de la cuenta.

Cualquier memorando escrito a mano por el corredor mostrando por que esa inversión pude ser buena para usted. Muestra la otra cara de la nota.

Cualquier articulo de cualquier publicación mostrando que su inversión tiene mayor riesgo o es más agresiva de lo que el formato de la cuenta declara y en cual usted debe reinvertir. Muestra el otro lado del articulo. Estos son solo pocos ejemplos de como usted puede desempeñarse con fuerza en la mediación.

CAPITULO 12

PREGUNTAS FRECUENTES DE INVERSIONISTAS.

En los pasados doce años, he sido autor financiero y columnista. Yo he escrito muchas columnas y artículos para periódicos y revistas de como resolver disputas de inversión, arbitraje de títulos valores, y los derechos del inversionista. Yo he recibidos muchas preguntas de inversionistas inquietos. A continuación están las preguntas más comunes y sus preocupaciones y su importancia. Donde es aplicable yo incluí fallos y arbitrajes reales que se ajustan a la pregunta.

PREGUNTA
Yo recibo llamadas de muchos corredores que desean mis negocios. Todos ellos me ofrecen el mejor servicio a buen precio. Un corredor en particular dijo que él trabajaba para una gran compañía nacional y que era un especialista en bonos, y dijo que había sido entrenado y totalmente competente para manejar grandes cantidades de dinero neto en particulares. Puedo creer que si una persona trabaja para una gran compañía, él es entrenado y competente en lo que esta haciendo?

RESPUESTA
Cuando yo trabaje para Dean Witter en 1994, el programa de entrenamiento para corredores fue de tres meses preparándose para la licencia series 7, además se aprenden los diferentes productos que la compañía vende. Hoy la industria ha llegado a ser tan competitiva y costosa que quieren que el corredor comience a llamar en frió a los clientes potenciales lo más pronto posible. Tiempo, experiencia y aprendizaje de otros agentes ayuda al agente a ser competente. No hay seguridad de que un agente trabajando para una gran compañía sea competente u honesto con la información que él le esta suministrando.

Como en el caso F.B. contra la firma corredora y el agente. Los árbitros fallaron a favor del demandante no solo la indemnización sino también daños punitivos relativos a la conducta del corredor con la cuenta del cliente. Los árbitros consideraron que el agente no era competente por las siguientes razones:

El agente testifico que en su opinión, el margen no incrementaba el riesgo.

EL agente testifico repetidamente que ella considero que la operación era una inversión lucrativa si su resultado en ganancia neta realizado (sin considerar el factor de que se pueden dar perdidas irreales).

El agente testifico que ella permitió que las perdidas siguieran corriendo (a pesar del entrenamiento activo). Por que las acciones "siempre regresan"

Los árbitros también consideraron que el corredor fue deshonesto y desviado por las siguientes razones:

Revisando deliberadamente todos los cuadros de los objetivos de la inversión para burlar una adecuada supervisión.

Entrando un valor de un millón neto en los documentos de una cuenta nueva a una firma diferente para crear la impresión de un cliente ingenuo.

Falsificando la experiencia en opciones para crear una gran libertad en el negocio.

Un reporte de cuenta engañoso con resultados calculados cada dos meses mostrando una ganancia total y ofreciendo retorno en la cuenta.

PREGUNTA

Yo le compre a mi corredor un bono sin cupones. Cuando yo pregunte cuál seria la comisión, él me dijo que seria más del uno por ciento, que era aceptable. Dos semanas después mi informe de cuenta llego. La cantidad de dinero que yo pague por los bonos fue un poquito menos del 5%. Las tasas de interés no se han alterado en las ultimas dos semanas entonces supe que no fue la fluctuación en los precios del bono sino en la comisión. Yo tengo algún recurso si el corredor me dice un precio sin embargo me cobra más?

RESPUESTA

Los bonos son comprados y vendidos "netos" con una rebaja o un sobreprecio. Esto significa que la comisión que usted paga esta incluida en el precio de los bonos. No existe una forma de usted pueda saber la comisión real que es cobrada diferente a las transacciones con acciones o fondos mutuos. Su problema es que probablemente su corredor le dio el precio de la comisión en el valor nominal de los bonos, no la cantidad de dinero que usted realmente esta pagando. Uno por ciento del valor nominal puede ser cinco por ciento o más en valor de un bono de descuento. Como su bono sin cupones. Un ejemplo, Un bono de $100,000.00 con $1,000.00 en comisión es uno por ciento. Pero un $100,000.00 bono sin cupón que se madura en veinticinco años puede costar $20,000.00. Ahora los $1,000.00 de comisión es el cinco por ciento de su costo actual que puede ser una comisión excesiva.

B.C. contra la firma corredora de bolsa.

El demandante compro $60,000.00 valor nominal en bonos del tesoro sin cupones, con vencimiento en treinta años. Ya que el precio de los bonos fue solo una fracción del valor nominal, el demandante sintió que fue demasiado $600.00 de comisión. Los árbitros estuvieron de acuerdo. Noviembre, 1989, New York.

PREGUNTA

Mi corredor me esta recomendando que venda el fondo mutuo en que yo estoy y compre otro que se esta desempeñando mejor. Él me dijo que habría un cobro por la venta cuando yo compro el nuevo fondo. Él desea que yo le firme algo llamado "carta de cambio"Puede darme usted un consejo en lo que yo debo firmar?

RESPUESTA

Su corredor esta siguiendo el procedimiento adecuado. Cuando se cambian fondos de familias diferentes una carta de cambio declara que usted entendió que existe un cargo de venta envuelto cuando se vende un fondo y se compra otro diferente. También puede declarar si sus objetivos de inversión se ajustan al nuevo bono, y usted esta cambiando porque su corredor dice que usted no lo puede conseguir en la misma familia de fondos para cumplir sus nuevos objetivos.

PREGUNTA

Yo soy una viuda de 71 años y vivo de los activos que herede de mi esposo fueron considerables. Mi agente es el mismo que mi esposo empleaba cuando él vivía y confiaba absolutamente en él. Dos años atrás mi agente me recomendó que él diera el poder para manejar los negocios de mi cuenta. Esto tiene sentido ya que yo nunca entendí nada de títulos valores. Él compraba y vendía, entonces no había razón para que él me llamara antes de cada negocio. Inclusive sin yo entender los informes de cuenta que el agente me enviaba, yo podía ver que mi patrimonio estaba disminuyendo cada mes en el ultimo año, y mi patrimonio ha disminuido en $60,000.00. Cometí un error dándole a él el poder? Debo ver a un abogado?

RESPUESTA

Su abogado no ha valorado la confianza que su esposo puso en él. Raramente en necesario para un inversionista darle el poder a un abogado. Usted debe tomar la ultima decisión sobre su cuenta. Si usted no entiende todos los factores de la transacción que su agente esta recomendando, haga una cita para verlo en persona y haga que el se lo explique mejor. Si usted aun no puede entender sus recomendaciones, sin embargo su estrategia muy sofisticada para una mujer de su edad y objetivos de inversión. Pregúntele a él que el de un folleto o perspectiva y llévelo a otro corredor o su contador por su opinión. Usted a lo mejor puede recuperar daños por el tipo de negociación que él prometió. En el caso T.& P.T. contra la firma corredora de bolsa y agentes, un tribunal de arbitramento fallo a favor de los daños que el demandante sufrió debido a los negocios que ejecuto el agente en opciones y títulos consiguiente al poder que tenia. Diciembre, 1989, Florida.

PREGUNTA

Yo herede cuando mi esposo falleció bonos municipales que él había comprado. Cuando ellos se vencieron no fue posible conseguir un precio alto, entonces el corredor me dijo que debería cambiar a margen entonces yo podía comprar casi tres veces más la cantidad de bonos, sin embargo generar gran ingreso. Él dijo eso porque los bonos eran de la mejor calidad, yo estaba completamente protegida. Recientemente yo recibí un telegrama del margen y debido a que yo no-tenia el dinero para pagar la factura del margen. La firma corredora liquido muchos de mis bonos. Ahora el valor de mi cuenta es mucho menor de lo que yo había comprado recientemente compre al precio más bajo. Que sucedió, fue un fraude?

RESPUESTA

Sin importar que tan conservadora sea la inversión, una vez es comprada en margen asume sustancialmente más riesgo. Margen es cuando usted presta dinero de la firma corredora de bolsa y usa sus títulos como garantía para comprar más títulos. Uno de los factores que afecta el valor de los bonos es la tasa de interés. Si la tasa de interés sube el precio de sus bonos bajara. Con bonos de calidad, usted puede comprar en margen casi tres veces el valor del bono original, esto significa que si el valor de sus bonos cae $1,000.00, en margen el valor de su cuenta puede bajar en $3,000.00. Si el valor de los bonos baja demasiado, la firma corredora de bolsa puede requerir más dinero o ellos pueden liquidar algunos de sus bonos para cubrir la llamada de mantenimiento de margen. En el caso de arbitraje R.S. contra la firma corredora de bolsa, el tribunal dio el fallo al demandante donde la falta de consejo del riesgo en el negocio de los bonos en margen fue un factor. Septiembre, 199, Florida.

PREGUNTA

Mi esposo y yo queremos retirarnos el próximo año. Dos años atrás nuestro agente le vendió a mi esposo algunas acciones que su firma coloco, y le garantizaron que no crecería menos de 10% en un corto periodo de tiempo. Aunque no estábamos buscando un crecimiento rápido y preguntamos si esas acciones eran apropiadas para nosotros él dijo que no podíamos perder. Esta emisión rápidamente bajo a la mitad del precio que pagamos por ellas. Podemos emprender un proceso judicial contra el corredor y su firma sabiendo que le entregamos y le dejamos vender nuestras acciones?.

RESPUESTA
Si estos títulos fueron inapropiados para usted por su edad, situación financiera y objetivos de inversión el agente no se los debió haber recomendado en primer lugar. Además Si usted estaba inconforme con esta meta de crecer rápido, el no los debió haber presionado con estas acciones. En los casos de arbitraje en la NASD el panel fallo a favor del demandante y encontró al agente y la firma responsable por la venta de inapropiados títulos valores colocados por la firma, Junio, 1991, Florida.

PREGUNTA
Cuando mi esposo murió a la edad de 74 años, su agente, con el que él llegó a ser muy buenos amigos y luego se convirtió en mi agente. En los años siguientes, el no solo me asistí con mi inversión también me ayudo a organizar mis finanzas y pagar mis cuentas, tanto como llevarme hasta la puerta de la oficina del doctor. Dos años atrás él me solicito un crédito de $50,000.00 que yo pensé era a corto plazo. El todavía no me ha pagado el dinero y dice que fue un regalo. Puedo emprender un proceso judicial para recuperar mis $50,000.00?

RESPUESTA.
Parece que su corredor tomo ventaja de su situación vulnerable. El no le debió haber solicitado dinero prestado, sin resistir ninguna asistencia que él le presto con las finanzas o patrocinar en otras áreas. En L.W.&T.B. contra la casa de valores, un tribunal de arbitramento encontró el agente responsable por venderle al cliente inversiones inapropi-

adas (con limitada asociación y opciones y fondos de ingresos) un robo civil en relación con su influencia sobre el demandante para entregarle cheques a él. El demandante gano el caso de daños triples contra el agente por el cargo de robo civil.

PREGUNTA
Yo compre una sociedad en comandita y algunos fondos a una firma corredora de bolsa. A pesar de que el agente me dio una proyección de los fondos y de la sociedad, el no explico que es casi imposible o que tenia una gran comisión en los fondos y que es una inversión de baja calidad en bono y acciones. ¿Cómo me dio la perspectiva y no me queje en ese momento, eso me disminuye las posibilidades en un caso de arbitramento ahora?

RESPUESTA
No, EL recibir una proyección o no diligenciar el arbitramento en ese momento no necesariamente excluye al inversionista para que pueda recuperar de la casa de valores su dinero por una inversión inadecuada. En el gremio de la bolsa de valores existe la Regla 405 "conozca a su cliente". Solo porque el agente le dio la información en la inversión no significa que usted ella se ajuste a sus necesidades.
En el caso B.& J.G. contra la firma corredora de bolsa, el demandante que había recibido una proyección recupero su dinero basado en inversión inadecuada e incumplimiento del agente al explicar el riesgo envuelto en la compra de la inversión. Florida, 1989

PREGUNTA
Yo no se nada de títulos valores entonces dependo de los consejos de mi agente. Sin embargo yo estoy encontrando que se hacen frecuentes negocios en mi cuenta. Muchos de los recibos de compra y venta que recibo no muestran la comisión. Significa esto que no me cuesta nada el que mi agente haga esos negocios? Este es el tipo de negocios aconsejable para una persona retirada?

RESPUESTA

Parece que existe un negocio excesivo, o múltiples negocios en su cuenta. Solo por que usted no ve la comisión como cantidad de dólares en la confirmación no significa que el corredor no haga dinero con el negocio. Los corredores no deben hacer negocios en su cuenta hasta que no le haya explicado completamente la transacción y usted le haya dado la aprobación. En el caso entre HS y GKS&Co. La firma corredora de bolsa fue encontrada culpable por comercio inautorizado en la cuenta de los clientes y los dineros fueron devueltos al demandante. Agosto, 1990, Florida.

PREGUNTA

Por que yo soy una viuda y vivo del Seguro Social y del ingreso de mis inversiones Mi agente me recomendó un fondo de alto ingreso cuando mi esposo murió en 1988. El fondo subió y bajo fue frecuentemente y sin embargo produjo relativamente alto interés. Yo no me siento cómoda viendo el valor de mi dinero cambiar todo el tiempo. Sin embargo yo no puedo salirme del fondo y recupera mi capital. Hay algo que yo pueda hacer?

RESPUESTA

Si su agente omitió el factor de que su dinero puede tener fluctuaciones sustanciales, usted puede tener un derecho de motivo legal. En un caso donde la demandante fue una viuda buscando "seguridad" las alternativas de bajo riesgo son los CDs. La demandante alego que el agente falsifico y omitió factores materiales en el alto ingreso gubernamental donde el cliente sufrió una sustancial perdida de capital. El panel de arbitramento retorno una sustancial suma de dinero al demandante. Florida, 1991.

PREGUNTA

El año pasado yo vendí mi casa y tenia $100,000.00 para invertir. Yo le dije a mi agente que deseaba ingreso y crecer. LE me recomendó dividir el dinero en dos fondos mutuos. ÉL me dijo cuales serian las comisiones y el rendimiento que recibiría en mi dinero. Yo estuve de acuerdo en comprar los fondos. Ahora me doy cuento que pude ahorrar $1,000.00 en la comisión si mi corredor me pone en el mismo tipo de fondo y en la misma familia de fondos. EL agente me debió haber dicho sobre este descuento?.

RESPUESTA

El agente tiene la obligación moral pero no es un requisito legal informarla sobre este descuento, conocido como punto de ruptura.
Aquí hay un caso de arbitraje donde los puntos de ruptura fueron un factor: In H.F. contra E.K. Group Securities, HF. Alego que el demandado fallo al informarle al cliente el precio de ruptura al que tenia derecho. Los arbitro fallaron a favor del demandante H.F. $1,305.00. Octubre, 1989, Florida.

PREGUNTA

Mi corredor me llamo sobre un fondo mutuo nuevo que su firma estaba vendiendo. Él dijo que podría ser manejada como una acción y me daría un enteres mensual. Lo que me intereso fue que él dijo que los podía comprar y sin tener que pagar comisión. Yo sé que el corredor tiene que hacer comisión para poder vivir y las firmas corredoras de bolsa no hacen nada gratis. Puede usted explicarme que es esto?

RESPUESTA

El corredor desea venderle un bono cerrado que esta teniendo su oferta inicial al público. Es verdad que usted no esta directamente pagando la comisión del corredor. Él recibe su parao de la firma corredora de bolsa por hacer la oferta al público. El problema es que el valor de los activos netos en cada cuota que esta comprando será menor al que usted esta pagando. Recuerde, fondos cerrados tienen dos precios; el valor del mercado, que seria el precio que usted en que usted lo compra o lo vende; y el valor neto del activo (VNA)que seria el precio real de cada cuota. Usted también debe entender que usted no recibe su primer cheque sino hasta después de 90 días porque el fondo tiene que ir al mercado abierto a comprar los bonos y eso toma tiempo. En ves de comprar este nuevo fondo se sentirá más cómodo comprando un fondo cerrado que haya estado en el mercado por seis meses o un año. De esta forma usted no tiene que esperar 90 días por su primer pago. Además probablemente no habrá una gran diferencia entre el valor del mercado y el VAN.

PREGUNTA
Acabe de recibir mi informe de fin de año de mi firma corredora de bolsa. Yo lo compare con mi cuenta, cosa que hago cada año y así puedo hacer mis impuestos. Él me advirtió de perdidas, de las que yo no tenia ni idea. Mi agente nunca me dijo de estas perdidas o transacciones que resultaron en estas perdidas. Cuando yo llame a mi corredor y le solicite que me explicara estos negocios él me dijo que habíamos discutido cada uno de ellos. Eso simplemente no es cierto. Que recurso tengo yo?

RESPUESTA
El informe de fin de año de las firmas corredoras es un excelente resumen para revisar todas las transacciones del año y sus valores. Existe una manera rápida de informarse de ganancias o perdidas sin mirar cada una de las confirmaciones de compra y venta. Si usted siente que hay transacciones que no fueron autorizadas por usted, entonces usted tiene recurso contra el agente si usted puede probar que no las autorizo.
W.R. y B.R. contra Merril Lynch. El demandante alega Merrill Lynch fallo en el seguimiento de las instrucciones del negocio, y llevo a cabo negocio no autorizados. Merrill Lynch negó la acusación y declaro que el demandante autorizo ratifico todos los negocios. Los árbitros fallaron a favor del demandante. Febrero 1990, Florida.

PREGUNTA
Estoy enojada. Mi agente me recomendó un fondo de bono de alto rendimiento. Yo no entendí cuál fue el riesgo. Cuando yo comprendí el riesgo que tenia yo lo vendí y perdí $2,600.00. EL corredor y la firma me dicen que no

hay nada que ellos puedan hacer. Yo fui donde el abogado y me dice que no es suficiente dinero para él o probablemente cualquier abogado tomar el caso. Que puedo hacer? Por favor ayúdeme.

RESPUESTA
Usted puede hacer algo. Primero, usted no necesita un abogado para radicar un arbitraje. Comuníquese con The National Association of Securities Dealers al 212-858-4000. Ellos le enviaran la información y formas que usted necesita diligenciar. Segundo, La N.A.S.D. tiene lo que es llamado "arbitraje simplificado"que es para demandas de $25,000.00 o menos. El costo para usted es menor que el de un arbitraje con un tribunal de arbitro, Muchos casos son radicados por arbitraje simple.

Un ejemplo: J & CF contra Kidder Peabody & company. El cliente alega que el corredor fallo en las instrucciones para vender fondos mutuos. Él demando por $1,280.00 y gano 1,025.00. Agosto, 1989. Los Ángeles, Ca.

Printed in the United States
42436LVS00002B/319-321